VERMONT WILDLIFE VIEWING GUIDE

Cindy Kilgore Brown

FALCON™

Helena, Montana

ACKNOWLEDGMENTS

This book represents the comments, suggestions, wisdom, expertise, thoughts, wishes, observations, considerations, and principles of a variety of people concerned about wildlife in Vermont. The list of those who contributed to this project far exceed the number of pages herein. First and foremost, many thanks to the Vermont Watchable Wildlife Steering Committee, and in particular, to Mary Jeanne Packer of the Green Mountain National Forest, whose dynamics and sheer determination pushed this project from dream to reality; Kate Davies, Defenders of Wildlife; Eric Goodenough, Ducks Unlimited; Steve Faccio, Vermont Institute of Natural Science; Juanita Blaskowski, Missisquoi National Wildlife Refuge; Gina Campoli, Vermont Agency of Natural Resources; Mark Scott, Vermont Fish and Wildlife; Charles Johnson, Vermont Forests, Parks and Recreation; and Mark Rosenthal, U.S. Army Corps of Engineers.

Additional thanks to the folks who reviewed and added material to the manuscript at various stages: Clay Grove, Adrien Villaruz, Frank Thompson, Bruce Flewelling, Bruce Reid, Mike Burbank, Chris Casey, Michael Schrotz, Beth LeClair, and Paul Lundberg; and to all the others at the Green Mountain National Forest in Rutland, Manchester, Rochester, and Middlebury, who gave me their time, thoughts, and good energy all along the way.

I am grateful to Len Gerardi, Ron Regan, Cedric Alexander, Bill Crenshaw, Tom Myers, Steve Parren, John Hall, Dan Marchant, Frank Snow, Kim Royar, Doug Blodgett, and John Buck and all the wildlife biologists who left only their initials and comments behind on the manuscript from the VT Department of Fish and Wildlife; Chuck Woessner and Bruce Amsden with the VT Department of Forests, Parks and Recreation; Peggy Struhsacker, Lamoille County Natural Resources Conservation District; Steve Swinburn, Central Vermont Public Service; John Ragonese, New England Power Company; Diana Osborne and Al Zelley, U.S. Fish and Wildlife; Bat Conservation International; Greg Knoettner, Appalachian Trail Conference; Pieter Straub and the Vermont Rabies Hotline.

For support from a distance, yet felt nonetheless: Terry Hoffman, Green Mountain National Forest Supervisor; Al Elser, VT Fish and Wildlife Commissioner; and Jim Cole, Wasatch-Cache National Forest.

To a special support group (for keeping me sane): Michael Cunningham and Farley Mowat II; Bill and Keefer Irwin; Pamela Rooney, U.S. Fish and Wildlife Service; Markly Wilson; and the National Watchable Wildlife folks.

And finally, to the production crew, who made all these thoughts and images come to print: Bill Schneider and John Grassy, Falcon Press; the multi-talented Reed Prescott III; the VT photographers, my comrades-n-chrome, Steve Faccio, Charles Willey, Jim Blakeslee, Richard Piliero, Susan Morse, Russell Hansen, Ted Levin, and Blake Gardner.

Author and State Project Manager
Cindy Kilgore Brown

Wildlife Viewing Guide Program Manager
Kate Davies, Defenders of Wildlife

Illustrations
Reed Prescott III

Front cover photo
Moose, CHARLES H. WILLEY

Back cover photo
Osmore Pond, Groton State Forest, MARGARET YOUNG
Belted kingfisher, STEVE FACCIO

CONTENTS

Project Sponsors 5

State Map 8

Introduction 9

National Watchable Wildlife Program 9

Viewing Tips and Outdoor Ethics 10

Rabies 11

How to Use this Guide 11

REGION ONE: SOUTHERN

Regional map 13

Site 1   Vernon, Bellows Falls, and Wilder Dams 14

Site 2   Bennington Fish Culure Station 15

Site 3   Branch Pond 16

Site 4   Grout Pond 17

Wild Animal Stories: Tracks and Signs 18

Site 5   Townshend Lake 20

Site 6   Gale Meadows Pond 21

Site 7   Otter Creek Wildlife Management Area 22

Site 8   Springfield Lake 23

Site 9   White Rocks National Recreation Area: Ice Beds Trails 24

Site 10   North Hartland Lake 24

Site 11   Vermont Institute of Natural Science 25

Site 12   Appalachian Trail: Dana Hill Field 26

Site 13   Appalachian Trail: Gifford Woods State Park 26

Site 14   Leffert's Pond 27

Site 15   Peavine 28

Site 16   White River National Fish Hatchery 29

REGION TWO: CENTRAL

Regional map 30

Site 17   Union Village Mystery Trail 31

Site 18   Podunk Wildlife Management Area 32

Site 19   Miller Pond 32

Site 20   Mount Horrid 33

Vermont's Natural Heritage 34

Site 21   Blueberry Hill Management Area 35

Site 22   Cornwall Swamp Wildlife Management Area 35

Site 23   Robert Frost Interpretive Trail 36

Site 24   West Hill 37

Site 25   Granville Gulf Reservation 37

Site 26   Dead Creek Wildlife Management Area 38

Site 27   Winona Lake (Bristol Pond) 39

Site 28   Lamoille County Nature Center 39

Site 29   Smugglers Notch State Park 40

REGION THREE: NORTHEAST KINGDOM

Regional map 41

Site 30   Groton State Forest 42

Site 31   Steam Mill Brook Wildlife Management Area 43

Site 32   Victory Basin Wildlife Management Area 44

Site 33   Maidstone State Park 45

Site 34   Route 114 45

Site 35   Wenlock Wildlife Management Area 46

Site 36   Mount Pisgah 47

Predators and Prey 48
Site 37   Willoughby Falls, Willoughby Falls Wildlife
             Management Area 49
Site 38   South Bay Wildlife Management Area 50
Site 39   Bill Sladyk Wildlife Management Area:
             Holland Pond Access 51
Site 40   Bill Sladyk Wildlife Management Area: Rt. 114 Access 52

REGION FOUR: NORTHWEST LAKE
Regional map 53
Site 41   The Birds of Vermont Museum 54
Site 42   Green Mountain Audubon Nature Center 54
Site 43   Malletts Bay State Park 55
Site 44   Sand Bar Wildlife Management Area 56
Not-So-Hidden Treasure: Vermont Wetlands 57
Site 45   Ed Weed Fish Culture Station 58
Site 46   Arrowhead Mountain Lake 59
Site 47   Fairfield Swamp Wildlife Management Area 60
Site 48   Lake Carmi State Park 60
Site 49   Missisquoi National Wildlife Refuge 61
Site 50   Shad Island and Bird's Foot Delta 62

Wildlife Index 63
Additional Reading 63

Much of Vermont's landscape was formed by erosion from wind, water, and glacial ice. One of the many natural attractions easily accessible to the public is Moss Glen Falls, located along Route 100 in the Granville Gulf Reservation.

BLAKE GARDNER

PROJECT SPONSORS

DEFENDERS OF WILDLIFE is a national, nonprofit organization of more than 80,000 members and supporters dedicated to preserving the natural abundance and diversity of wildlife and its habitat. A one-year membership is $20 and includes six issues of *Defenders,* an award-winning conservation magazine, and *Wildlife Advocate*, an activist-oriented newsletter. To join or for further information, write or call Defenders of Wildlife, 1101 14th Street NW, Suite 1400, Washington, DC 20005, (202) 682-9400.

The FOREST SERVICE, U.S. DEPARTMENT OF AGRICULTURE, manages the resources of the Green Mountain National Forest—Vermont's only national forest—under the concepts of ecosystem management and sustainable multiple use to meet the diverse needs of people. The Green Mountain National Forest is proud to sponsor this program in order to promote awareness and enjoyment of fish and wildlife on national forest lands. USDA Forest Service, The Green Mountain National Forest, 231 North Main Street, Rutland, Vermont 05701. TPY phone number : 747-6765.

The U.S. FISH AND WILDLIFE SERVICE, REGION 5 programs include the national wildlife refuge system, protection of threatened and endangered species, conservation of migratory birds, fisheries restoration, recreation/education, wildlife research, private landowner technical assistance and partnerships, and law enforcement. Help acquire and conserve wildlife refuge habitat by purchasing Federal Duck Stamps. For more information, contact U. S. Fish and Wildlife Service, 300 Westgate Center Drive, Hadley, Massachusetts 01035-9589; Phone: 413-253-8563

The NATIONAL FISH AND WILDLIFE FOUNDATION, chartered by Congress to stimulate private giving to conservation, is an independent not-for-profit organization. Using federally funded challenge grants, it forges partnerships between the public and private sectors to conserve the nation's fish, wildlife, and plants. National Fish and Wildlife Foundation, 1120 Connecticut Avenue, Washington, D.C. 20036 (202) 857-0166.

The DEPARTMENT OF DEFENSE is the steward of about 25 million acres of land in the United States, many of which possess irreplaceable natural and cultural resources. The DoD is pleased to support the Watchable Wildlife program through its Legacy Resource Management Program, a special initiative to enhance the conservation and restoration of natural and cultural resources on military land. For more information, contact the Office of the Deputy Assistant Secretary of Defense (Environment), 400 Army Navy Drive, Suite 206, Arlington, VA 22202-2884.

 The NATIONAL PARK SERVICE is charged with administering the units of the National Park System in a manner that protects and conserves their natural and cultural resources for the enjoyment of present and future generations. For more information, contact the National Park Service, P.O. Box 37127, Washington, D.C. 20013-7127.

   The VERMONT AGENCY OF NATURAL RESOURCES is responsible for managing and protecting the integrity, diversity, and vitality of Vermont's natural resources. The agency is organized into three departments: Fish and Wildlife; Forests, Parks and Recreation; and Environmental Conservation. The Department of Fish and Wildlife is responsible for the conservation of all Vermont species of fish and wildlife and their habitats. The Department of Forests, Parks and Recreation provides public lands, assists landowners, and offers conservation education in order to sustain Vermont's forests and their resources. The Department of Environmental Conservation manages air and water quality as well as solid and hazardous wastes. For more information, write or call 103 South Main Street, Waterbury, Vermont 05671-0301. Phone: 241-3700.

Copyright © 1994 by Falcon Press Publishing Co., Inc., Helena and Billings, MT.
Illustrations copyright © 1994 by Defenders of Wildlife.
Published in cooperation with Defenders of Wildlife.

Defenders of Wildlife and its design are registered marks of Defenders of Wildlife, Washington, D.C.

FALCON™

Design, typesetting, and other prepress work by Falcon Press, Helena, Montana.

Printed in Korea.

Cataloging-in-Publication Data
Brown, Cindy Kilgore
    Vermont wildlife viewing guide / Cindy Kilgore Brown.
        p.   cm. --(Watchable wildlife series)
    Includes bibliographical references and index.
    ISBN 1-56044-291-3
        1. Wildlife viewing sites--Vermont--Guidebooks. 2. Wildlife watching--Vermont--Guidebooks. 3. Vermont--Guidebooks   I. Title.
II. Series.
QL 209.B76 1994
508.743--dc20
                                              94-19270
                                              CIP

State of Vermont
OFFICE OF THE GOVERNOR
Montpelier 05609

Tel.: (802) 828-3333
Fax: (802) 828-3339
TDD: (802) 828-3345

Welcome to the world of Vermont wildlife!

Many visitors to our state are familiar with the quintessential Vermont scene of picturesque villages and Holsteins complacently roaming through a lush hillside meadow. But there is more beauty in the Vermont landscape than is readily apparent. Hidden in the wetland grasses along Lake Champlain, deep within the canopy of the Green Mountain forest, and gliding along meandering rivers and rushing mountain streams is a precious world of Vermont wildlife.

The *Vermont Wildlife Viewing Guide* will help reveal the secrets around us. White-tailed deer and black bears, peregrine falcons and loons, a symphony of songbirds too numerous to name, are but a few of the species of wildlife in Vermont that entertain and delight viewers. This guide explains where to go in the state to catch a glimpse, hear a call, or see a sign of these special treasures. There are not only directions on how to get there and what to look for, but also information on how the animals survive and interact with their habitats.

Vermont ranks highest among the lower 48 states in the number of residents who enjoy observing, feeding, photographing wildlife and/or go hunting. The *Vermont Wildlife Viewing Guide* is an invitation for you to join those many Vermonters across the state in appreciating and understanding the creatures around us and the environment we share.

I hope you enjoy this book and the wildlife resources of Vermont.

Sincerely,

Howard Dean, M. D.
Governor

VERMONT

Wildlife Viewing Areas

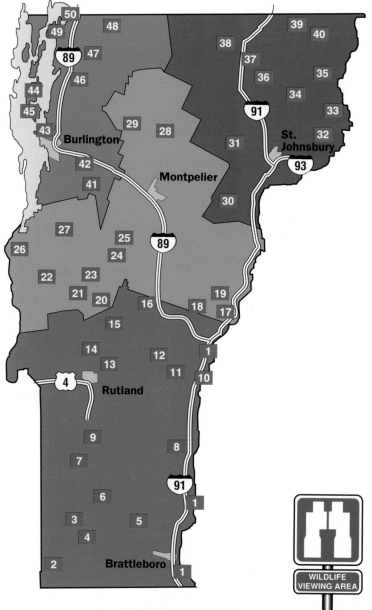

HIGHWAY SIGNS

As you travel in Vermont and other states, look for these special highway signs that identify wildlife viewing sites. These signs will help guide you to the viewing area. NOTE: Be sure to read the written directions provided with each site in this book — highway signs may refer to more than one site along a particular route.

INTRODUCTION

To mention Vermont is to summon a host of scenes. Some people think of white farmhouses and rich, green meadows. For others, autumn's brilliant colors come to mind, and perhaps a covered bridge over a clear stream. There are scenes of fly fishing on the Batten Kill River, of snowshoeing and skiing, fishing, hiking, and hunting—all in the spectacular setting that is Vermont.

In all seasons and corners of the state, Vermont is equally rich in scenes of wildlife. Visit a wetlands complex just before nightfall and you can witness the ponderous grace of a 1,000-pound bull moose browsing on sedges. The common loon's haunting voice breaks the morning stillness on many Vermont lakes and ponds. You can see the colorful flash of a scarlet tanager, and, with a bit of luck, the shadow of a northern goshawk on the wing. There are 247 species of birds which spend all or part of the year in Vermont, and 58 species of mammals, from the massive moose to the dimunitive pygmy shrew. Vermont's seemingly endless array of rivers, lakes, and streams support 88 fish species, from rainbow trout to largemouth bass and northern pike.

This guide will lead you to 50 of Vermont's best wildlife viewing areas, places where animals feed, rest, migrate, and raise their young. Take some time to learn about the needs of wild animals, and their habits. Successful wildlife viewing requires patience and practice. The reward, often, is only a glimpse—the white flash of a deer's tail, a momentary look at a mink—but these images can last a lifetime. Savor the days you spend in the mountains and forests of Vermont, and the wildlife memories you make.

THE NATIONAL WATCHABLE WILDLIFE PROGRAM

The National Watchable Wildlife Program is a nationwide cooperative effort to combine wildlife conservation with America's growing interest in wildlife-related outdoor recreation. The program is founded on the notion that people, given opportunities to enjoy and learn about wildlife in a natural setting, will become advocates for conservation in the future.

The cornerstone of this program is the Watchable Wildlife Series™ of state-by-state wildlife viewing guides, of which Vermont is now a part. This book is much more than a guide: the viewing areas are part of a growing nationwide network. Travel routes to each site will be marked with the brown and white binoculars logo. Similar viewing networks have been established in 16 other states, with more planned in the coming years.

More than 110 viewing sites were nominated for inclusion in this book. Sites were rated according to accessibility, scenic qualities, ability to accomodate visitors, and for ecologically-diverse habitats that support a variety of free-roaming wildlife.

Publication of this guide is only the first step in Vermont's Watchable Wildlife effort. Enhancement of viewing sites through interpretive signs, trail maintenance, boardwalk or viewing platforms will be the next step.

Use this guide to plan outings that coincide with peak wildlife viewing opportunities. Consult it while traveling for interesting side trips. Take advantage of on-site education programs. And finally, support wildlife agencies and private efforts to fund and conserve wildlife programs by becoming an active partner in resource protection.

VIEWING TIPS AND OUTDOOR ETHICS

Much of the excitement of wildlife viewing stems from the fact that you can never be sure of what you will see. While many species are difficult to see under the best of circumstances, there are several things you can do to greatly increase your chances of seeing wild animals in their natural environs.

The cardinal rule of wildlife viewing is patience. You must spend enough time in the field. If you arrive at a viewing site expecting to see every species noted in this guide on your first visit, you will surely be disappointed. Review the tips below, and enjoy your viewing trips, regardless of what you see.

Visit when animals are active. The first and last hours of daylight are generally the best times to view wildlife. The majority of Vermont's mammals will only be seen during these hours.

Wildlife viewing is often seasonal. Many wildlife species are present only during certain times of year. Migrating waterfowl, for example, pass through Vermont in early spring and again in autumn. Moose and deer gather in sheltered areas for winter, then move into open areas in the warmer months. Each site account in this guide contains a wealth of information about optimal seasons for viewing selected species. Consult a field guide for additional information, or call the site owner for an update before you visit.

Learn to be still, silent and patient. Quick movements will scare wildlife. Take a few steps, then stop, look, and listen. Use your ears to locate birds or the movements of other animals. Walk into the wind if possible, avoiding brittle sticks and leaves. Use trees and vegetation as a blind. Your parked car, or a canoe, make good viewing blinds.

Use viewing aids. Binoculars are a necessity for maximum enjoyment of wildlife. Spotting scopes also bring the animals in closer and many have adapters to fit 35mm camera bodies.

Use field guides. Pocket field guides are essential for positive identification of the many animals named at each viewing site. Guides are available for virtually every plant and animal found in Vermont, and contain valuable information on where animals live, what they eat, and when they raise their young.

Leave your pets at home. Wild animals flee when dogs or other domestic animals enter their area. Pets can also chase, harass, or kill wildlife.

Prepare for your outing. Vermont is famous for shifting temperatures and conditions. Carry extra clothes in backpacks and in the car. Winter weather can be life threatening—take precautions, including car maintainence. Bring insect repellent in the summer months. Wear comfortable, sturdy shoes or hiking boots in the field. Review the site account in this guide before you visit, checking for warnings about road conditions and weather.

Enjoy wildlife from a distance. You can actually harm the wildlife you care about by getting too close. Move away from an animal if it stops feeding and raises its head sharply, appears nervous or aggressive, or changes its direction of travel. Refrain from touching or feeding animals. Leave seemingly abandoned wildlife, including young, alone. If you are concerned about an animal, contact a state game warden.

Honor the rights of private landowners. Always ask permission before entering private property. Leave no trace of your presence. **Honor the use of**

public lands by others. Many areas are marked as to whether snowmobiling, mountain biking, snowshoeing, or cross-country skiing are allowed. Most public lands are open to hunting and fishing. Hunting seasons may be noted in the Vermont Digest of Fish and Wildlife Laws, which may be obtained from the Vermont Fish and Wildlife Department.

Be aware of Eurasian Watermilfoil, a nuisance aquatic plant transmitted from pond to pond by plant fragments that have caught onto boats. Inspect all boats for vegetation before leaving an area. If any plant fragments are present, leave them on dry land away from the shoreline.

Hiking is discouraged on the higher elevations during mud season (April-May) as melting snow creates wet and muddy conditions. Hiking at this time damages trails.

RABIES

Rabies, a deadly disease, can infect all mammals, including humans. The red fox, raccoon, bat, skunk, and woodchuck are the most likely wildlife carriers. Rabies is caused by a virus found in the saliva and brain tissue of a rabid animal, and is most commonly transmitted by the bite of a rabid animal, or by contamination of a person's eyes, mouth, nose, or in an open cut or wound.

Be aware of any animal displaying unusual behavior—rabid animals may appear tame, aggressive, or paralyzed. Since some infected animals may appear perfectly normal, avoid picking up or handling any wild animal. Do not handle road-killed or other animal carcasses.

Contact the Vermont Rabies Hotline at 1-800-4-RABIES (1-800-472-2437) for more information about rabies, or if you see an animal with unusual or aggressive behavior.

HOW TO USE THIS GUIDE

This guide is divided into four chapters, each representing a region of Vermont: Southern, Central, Northwest Lakes, and the Northeast Kingdom. Shaded tabs on right-hand pages allow you to move quickly from one region to another. Each regional area begins with a full-color map showing major roads, towns, and site locations.

Each viewing site features a series of **wildlife icons**. These give a quick reference as to what types of animals are common within this specific area.

Below the icons is a **Description** of the site. This section offers information about the habitat and general wildlife information. The **Viewing Information** section offers additional notes on wildlife species and optimal times or locations for viewing selected animals. *NOTES OF CAUTION REGARDING TRAVEL RESTRICTIONS, HAZARDS, OR OTHER WARNINGS APPEAR IN CAPITAL LETTERS.*

Written **Directions** are given from the **Closest Town**, which is listed beneath the directions. This is the nearest town where gas, food and/or lodging is available. Always travel with an up-to-date Vermont road map and/or DeLorme's *Vermont Atlas and Gazetteer*, which is highly recommended for traveling Vermont's many backroads. When traveling to a viewing site, watch for the brown and white binocular sign.

Ownership refers to the agency or organization that owns or manages the site. A phone number is included and may be used for gaining additional information. **THE STATE-WIDE AREA CODE FOR VERMONT IS 802.** Abbreviations for ownerships appear below:

CVPS   Central Vermont Public Service

NEPCO   New England Power Company

ACE   U.S. Army Corps of Engineers

USFWS   U.S. Fish and Wildlife Service

USFS   USDA Forest Service (the Green Mountain National Forest)

VTFW   Vermont Department of Fish and Wildlife

VTFPR   Vermont Department of Forests, Parks and Recreation

Recreation and Facility Icons are located at the bottom of each viewing site. These icons include valuable information on parking, restrooms, fees, barrier-free access, and other items.

WILDLIFE ICONS

 songbirds

upland birds

waterfowl

wading birds

shorebirds

marine birds

birds of prey

small mammals

hoofed mammals

carnivores

freshwater mammals

fish

reptiles, amphibians

bats

wildflowers

FACILITIES AND RECREATION SYMBOLS

 Parking

 Restrooms Pit Toilets

Barrier-free

Picinic

Drinking Water

Entry Fee

 Camping

 Hiking

Cross-country Skiing

Snowshoeing

Appalachian Trail

Long Trail

 Boat Ramp

 Motorized Boats

Non-Motorized Boats

Fishing

Hunting

Horse Trails

Lodging

 Restaurants

Bicycling

Snowmobiling

REGION ONE: SOUTHERN

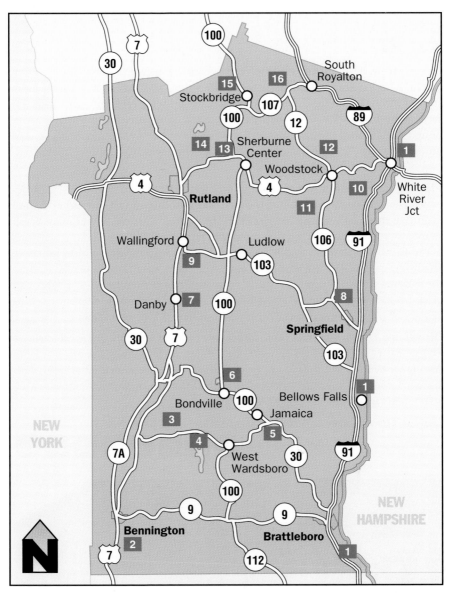

WILDLIFE VIEWING SITES
1. Vernon, Bellows Falls, and Wilder Dams
2. Bennington Fish Culture Station
3. Branch Pond
4. Grout Pond
5. Townshend Lake
6. Gale Meadows Pond
7. Otter Creek Wildlife Management Area
8. Springweather Nature Area, North Springfield Lake
9. White Rocks National Recreation Area: Ice Beds Trail
10. North Hartland Lake
11. Vermont Institute of Natural Science
12. Appalachian Trail: Dana Hill Field
13. Appalachian Trail: Gifford Woods State Park
14. Leffert's Pond
15. Peavine
16. White River National Fish Hatchery

1. VERNON, BELLOWS FALLS, AND WILDER DAMS

Description: These three hydroelectric dams have fish ladders, interpretive displays, and visitor centers open 9 a.m. to 5 p.m. May through October. Each station offers excellent displays interpreting Atlantic salmon restoration efforts. New England Power's fish ladders assist salmon on their journey from Long Island Sound to spawning locations as far as the Ammonoosic River, 270 miles upstream. Each fish ladder includes viewing windows, allowing observation of salmon and shad.

Viewing Information: To observe salmon on their return migration, visit between the last week of May and the first week of July. Adult salmon and shad negotiate these fish ladders on the final leg of their journey, which may begin as far away as the west coast of Greenland. Upstream from each dam, portions of the Connecticut River and its tributaries provide spawning habitat for these anadromous fish. During winter months, the open water which persists below these dams provides unique fishing opportunities for bald eagles. Eagles can often be seen during the morning hours and again in the late afternoons. Binoculars or a spotting scope are highly recommended for best viewing.

Directions: To reach Vernon Dam, follow Interstate 91 to Route 5. Travel north on Rt. 5 to Rt. 142. Follow Rt. 142 south for 7 miles. Bellows Falls Dam is located in downtown Bellows Falls off Rt. 5. To visit Wilder Dam, take exit 12 off I-91. Follow Rt. 5 north for 1.9 miles. Turn right onto Depot Street, then left onto Norwich Street, and right onto Passumpsic Avenue.

Closest Town: Vernon, Bellows Falls, Wilder   **Size:** NA

Ownership: NEPCO (603) 448-2200

At the three fish ladders, Atlantic salmon and shad pass through an entrance gate and move into a channel where they swim up a series of waterfalls and exit back into the Connecticut River. JOHN RAGONESE/NEW ENGLAND POWER

14

2. BENNINGTON FISH CULTURE STATION

Description: Constructed in 1916, Bennington is one of Vermont's oldest fish hatcheries. Primarily an outdoor facility, it consists of 16 dirt ponds with 31 raceways. Brook, brown, and rainbow trout are reared from egg to stream release size, measuring 9-12 inches in length. Approximately 400,000 trout are reared annually to be released in Vermont's streams, rivers, ponds, and lakes. Open daily 9 a.m. to 4 p.m. year-round.

Viewing Information: The best viewing here is from April to the end of June, and again in September and October. Visitors can examine fish at close range in raceways and ponds, and see them in different stages of growth. The brook trout is not a true trout, but rather a member of the char family. During its fall spawning period, the brook trout turns a brilliant red-orange color. It requires colder water than either the brown or rainbow trout. While fish are the focus here, it is not unusual to see mink, river otter, osprey, great blue heron, and belted kingfisher raiding the hatchery ponds for an easy meal.

Directions: From downtown Bennington at the four corners of Route 7 and Rt. 9, travel east 0.5 mile. Turn right at intersection of Beech and Main streets. Follow 0.4 mile to a Y-intersection and bear right onto South Stream Road. Continue 1.5 miles to hatchery.

Closest Town: Bennington

Ownership: VTFW 442-4556   **Size:** 250 acres

The brook trout, or "squaretail," the smallest of the native salmonids of Vermont, is actually a relative of the Arctic char. Spawning in the fall, it will build a redd of gravel in the shallows of cold-water ponds and lakes. FREDERICK PRADON

3. BRANCH POND

Description: Bordering the Lye Brook Wilderness in the Green Mountain National Forest, this site offers a variety of experiences, including easy canoe access and a nearby trailhead for the Appalachian Trail.

Viewing Information: This site presents opportunities to find signs and tracks of beaver, black bear, moose, bobcat, and river otter. The common loon is generally present in the summer months—be extremely careful not to disturb these sensitive birds. By canoe, one may encounter signs of beaver, as well as river otter and the elusive mink. Note the boggy islands with leatherleaf and pitcher plants. Watch for diving ducks such as the hooded merganser. Watch and listen for the colorful pileated woodpecker and the camouflaged ruffed grouse. In 1991, the USDA Forest Service and the Vermont Department of Fish and Wildlife released pine martens in the area—look for this tree-climbing member of the weasel family.

Directions: From Stratton, travel Forest Road 6 east into the national forest for 6.8 miles. During this stretch, there are several scenic wetlands and overlooks. Travel north on FR 70 for 2.1 miles to parking area.

Closest Town: Stratton

Ownership: USFS 362-2307

Size: 43 acres

The fisher's one-year gestation period is the longest of any North American mammal. Eight to twelve pounds of sheer energy, fishers are capable of leaping forty feet from one tree to another. Fearsome in combat, this weasel is the only natural predator of porcupines in Vermont.
CINDY KILGORE BROWN

16

4. GROUT POND

Description: This 79-acre pond is nestled in the northern hardwood and co-niferous forest of the Green Mountain National Forest, one of Vermont's most scenic areas. Visitors can explore 15 miles of hiking and cross-country ski trails, or canoe camp. The area feels secluded, but is only a half hour's drive from Stratton Mountain, a popular year-round resort. The site is part of a study on black bear habitat sponsored by the Vermont Department of Fish and Wild-life, the USDA Forest Service, and the Stratton Mountain Resort.

Viewing Information: Moose, black bear, bobcat, pine marten, beaver, snow-shoe hare, diving and dabbling ducks, and a variety of songbirds may be seen. The haunting cry of the common loon may be heard in the early morning. Moose browse aquatic plants. Watch for osprey feeding on the pond's healthy population of perch, bass, pickerel, sunfish, and bullhead. Along the access road is a shrub land community, maintained by prescribed fire for habitat di-versity; look for ruffed grouse, white-tailed deer, red fox, and wild turkey in this area.

Directions: From Stratton, travel FH 6 (also called W. Wardsboro-E. Arlington Road) in the Green Mountain National Forest. Follow 2 miles to pond access.

Closest Town: Stratton

Ownership: USFS 362-2307

Size: 1,513 acres

Overnight camping is one of the most enjoy-able ways to become acquainted with wildlife. In the dark, the sounds of nature become more apparent. Listen for the call of the common loon at sunset, a barred owl in the night, the splashing of a moose entering a pond at sunrise.

BLAKE GARDNER

Otter tracks and slide

Pileated woodpecker

Yellow-bellied sapsucker

Canada Goose

Beaver

Deer browse

WILD ANIMAL STORIES: TRACKS AND SIGNS

To catch a glimpse of a black bear, white-tailed deer, or bobcat is an exhilerating experience, made even more so by the rarity of the event. However, the signs left behind by these same animals—tracks, droppings (known as "scat"), browsed grass, and twigs—can be found throughout the forest. You need only know where to look and what to look for. "Tracking" an animal means knowing something about its habits and needs. What does the animal eat? What kind of cover requirements does it have? Is it an animal of the field or the forest?

The word "tracking" brings to mind imprints left behind in snow or mud. Tracks,

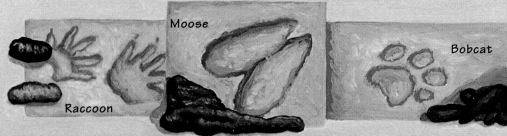

Moose

Bobcat

Raccoon

Raptor and prey

White-tailed deer

Bear claw on beech

Porcupine

Snowshoe hare

White-tailed buck rub

Mice

REED A. PRESCOTT

Cottontail browse

however, are just one of the many visible signs left by wildlife. In winter, deer commonly eat the bark of small hemlocks and striped maple trees. The resulting scars on young trees are permanent evidence that the area is important habitat for deer. Snowshoe hares nibble on small spruce boughs growing above the snow. The residual twig, clipped by the hare's sharp front teeth, looks as though it was cut cleanly with a pocket knife. Fox scat on a trail can show you what it ate recently. Identifying tracks and signs takes patience, a keen eye, and knowledge of your quarry, but the rewards of nature revealed are well worth the effort.

White-tailed deer

Snowshoe hare

Red fox

19

5. TOWNSHEND LAKE

Description: A parking area off Route 30 overlooks this 95-acre lake. This site provides an opportunity to view migrating waterfowl and birds of prey, including osprey and hawks. An Atlantic salmon trap is located below the dam, part of the anadromous fish restoration project on the Connecticut River.

Viewing Information: During spring and fall migrations, osprey, red-tailed and broad-winged hawk, northern raven, Canada goose, and a variety of waterfowl may be viewed almost any time of the day. Raptors often pass within 100 yards of the parking area. Look for signs of beaver activity in the water and along the shore. Early morning and early evening viewings are best during the summer. Binoculars or a spotting scope enhance viewing.

Directions: *From Brattleboro, travel north on Route 30 for 18 miles. Parking is on the left, approximately 0.25 mile beyond the project office.*

Closest Town: Townshend

Ownership: ACE 365-7703

Size: 1,010 acres

Diving ducks such as hooded mergansers take their food while swimming underwater. Their sharp, serrated bills enable them to hold onto struggling fish, frogs, and eels. These fast-flying cavity nesters prefer wooded sloughs, streams, and ponds in swamps.
STEVE FACCIO

6. GALE MEADOWS POND

Description: Gale Meadows, a 195-acre impoundment on Mill Brook in the towns of Londonderry and Winhall, is used by a variety of wildlife. Many waterfowl species nest here, including the wood duck, hooded merganser, and mallard. Great blue herons have recently nested on the pond, as well as common loons. The northern goshawk, American bittern, and saw-whet owl are also known to nest here. Mammals such as mink, beaver, and river otter frequent the pond and surrounding upland habitat. A white-tailed deer wintering area exists on the adjacent land. The pond supports many warm-water fish: largemouth bass, bluegill, pickerel, and yellow perch. Standing dead trees at the northern edge of the pond attract songbirds and waterfowl.

Viewing Information: Best viewing is from May through November; many species are most active during the early morning hours. Artificial nest boxes for wood ducks can be seen at the northern edge of the pond. Check the shallow waters for nesting bass and sunfish in late spring/early summer. *DO NOT DISTURB WATERFOWL DURING NESTING PERIOD, MAY/JUNE.*

Directions: *From Route 30 in Bondville, turn north on Coleman Road. Go approximately 0.75 mile to Tratell Road and turn left. Continue another mile and turn left onto Gale Meadow Access Road.*

Closest Town: Bondville   **Ownership:** VTFW 886-2215

Size: 400 acres, including pond

To build its lodge, a beaver will first pile branches together, then swim up underneath the pile to hollow out a central living quarter. A family of eight beavers requires one ton of bark to survive the winter. TED LEVIN

SOUTHERN

Description: This diverse site is located along the Mount Tabor-Danby line. Otter Creek, a major water course that winds along the western boundary, provides a good brook trout fishery. Some 800 acres of this site are forested, primarily with hardwoods. Wetlands located along the Otter Creek floodplain occupy about 260 acres. Open fields account for the remaining 65 acres.

Viewing Information: The combination of forest, field, and wetland habitats host a diversity of wildlife species, many of which may be seen from the parking area. April through October are best viewing months. Songbirds, such as the scarlet tanager, blackburnian warbler, and eastern wood pewee are especially active early mornings. Throughout the day, raptors such as the red-tailed hawk and northern harrier perch in dead trees along hedgerows and the creek. Late afternoon is the best time to see white-tailed deer in the fields, especially in early spring. Visitors on spring evenings may be able to hear the courtship calls of American woodcock in the cleared areas adjacent to the creek, 0.25-mile south of the parking area.

Directions: *From Rutland, travel south on Route 7. Management Area pull-off is located about 4.5 miles south of the village of South Wallingford on east side of Rt. 7. Pull-off is located 1 mile north of the Rt. 7 intersection of Mount Tabor village.*

Closest Town: Mount Tabor

Ownership: VTFW 483-2172

Size: 1,139 acres

Hawk migration occurs in autumn after the passing of a cold front, which provides the advantage of a good tail wind. In the spring, raptors appear to move on a warm front. All hawks, such as this red-tailed hawk, are protected by state and federal laws.
RUSSELL HANSEN

8. SPRINGWEATHER NATURE AREA, NORTH SPRINGFIELD LAKE

Description: This area includes 70 acres of fields, mixed forests, brooks, a small beaver pond, and a floodplain adjacent to a shallow reservoir behind the North Springfield Dam. Nature trails are provided; in winter, the area is groomed for snowmobiles. Cross-country skiing is also popular.

Viewing Information: Excellent birding opportunities, with 156 species recorded here. In fall, follow the trail west overlooking the lake to view sizeable numbers of migrating waterfowl, such as blue and green-winged teal and ring-necked duck. The common merganser, American black duck, wood duck, and mallard nest in the wetlands. Wading birds, such as the great blue and green-backed heron, are often seen. American kestrel, osprey, and other raptors, along with belted kingfisher, hunt the fields and waterways. Bald eagles have also been known to visit. Upland birds, such as American woodcock and ruffed grouse, may be sighted along the forest edge. Songbirds include the eastern bluebird, indigo bunting, scarlet tanager, ovenbird, and white-throated sparrow. Binoculars or a spotting scope recommended.

Directions: *From Springfield, follow Route 106 and Rt. 11 northwest. Continue on Rt. 106 north for 2.5 miles to the entrance of the North Springfield Dam on the right. Follow 0.8 mile and cross the dam. At stop sign, turn left and follow 0.6 mile to site on left.*

Ownership: ACE, 886-2775; leased to Ascutney Mountain Audubon Society

Closest Town: Springfield

Size: 70 acres

In search of prey, the belted kingfisher will hover over the water, then plunge-dive to seize a fish. Kingfishers will make their nests as deep as eight feet underground, lining the nest with feathers, grass, and fish scales.
STEVE FACCIO

9. WHITE ROCKS NATIONAL RECREATION AREA: ICE BEDS TRAIL

Description: This scenic trail boasts a large talus slope, panoramic views of the White Rocks cliffs, and mature red spruce and hemlock forests. Historically a nesting site for peregrine falcons, common ravens and turkey vultures also frequent these cliffs. Captive-bred peregrine falcons were reintroduced in the 1980s, and in recent years have again used the cliffs for roosting and nesting.

Viewing Information: Common raven may be seen year-round; best viewing of hawks and falcons occurs mid to late summer. The winter wren and blackburnian warbler, along with kinglets and juncos, may be found in the spruce forest spring through fall. Binoculars or spotting scope recommended.

Directions: *From Route 7 in Wallingford, go east on Rt. 140 for 3 miles. Bear right at sign for White Rocks NRA. Take the first right and follow signs to parking area. Follow Ice Bed Trail 0.6 mile to base of slopes.*

Closest Town: Wallingford   **Ownership:** USFS 362-2307

Size: 36,000 acres (White Rocks National Recreation Area)

10. NORTH HARTLAND LAKE

Description: From the top of North Hartland Lake's flood-control dam, an expanse of water, open field, and forested edge unfolds below. Migratory waterfowl, hawks, coyote, mink, wild turkey, white-tailed deer, and songbirds can be seen and heard. The spillway provides nesting sites for common ravens.

Viewing Information: Early morning or evening offers the best viewing, though white-tailed deer, wild turkey, common raven, and turkey vulture may be seen most anytime. Early mornings, listen for turkeys as they call to each other. In the evenings, whip-poor-wills can be heard. Common ravens nest in April and May. *CLIMBING ON THE FACE OF THE DAM IS PROHIBITED.*

Directions: *From White River Junction, travel approximately 5 miles south on Route 5 to Clay Hill Road. Turn right and travel 1.8 miles to entrance road. Park near office.*

Closest Town: White River Junction

Ownership: ACE 295-2855   **Size:** 1,405 acres

SOUTHERN

Description: The headquarters for the nonprofit environmental education and research organization, VINS includes a nature preserve, bird banding station, and raptor rehabilitation center. Trails free to the public pass through fields, hardwood and coniferous forests, and encircle a beaver pond. There is an entry fee to the Raptor Center, a living collection of owls, hawks, falcons, and eagles. Educational programs and field trips are offered year-round; a fee is charged. The gift shop features wildlife-related books, tapes, and educational games.

Viewing Information: Along the trails look for warblers, thrushes, bobolinks, tanagers, sharp-shinned hawk, American kestrel, barred owl, red-tailed hawk, beaver, and white-tailed deer. Around the pond search for spotted salamander, green and bull frog, garter snake, also painted and snapping turtle. The Raptor Center houses permanently disabled birds of prey in spacious outdoor flight habitats. Examine the sharp talons of a bald eagle, hear the hoot of a great horned owl, and spot a camouflaged screech owl just a few feet away; twenty-five species of these majestic birds can be viewed. Drop by the bird banding station any weekday morning during spring or fall to visit with staff and get a close-up look at a number of colorful songbirds.

Directions: *Turn off Route 4 at west end of the Green in downtown Woodstock (at large stone church) onto Church Hill Road. Follow 1.8 miles up road to VINS sign on right.*

Closest Town: Woodstock

Ownership: VINS 457-2779   **Size:** 77 acres

The Ice Beds Trail lies within the White Rocks National Recreation Area of the Green Mountain National Forest. This 36,400-acre tract preserves habitat for wildlife, and offers people opportunities for a backwoods recreational experience.

BLAKE GARDNER

12. APPALACHIAN TRAIL: DANA HILL FIELD

Description: The top of Dana Hill is an old pasture bordered on one side by ancient apple trees, on another by a pine plantation, and on a third by mixed hardwoods. The Appalachian Trail passes through the center of this area.

Viewing Information: Wild turkey and white-tailed deer feed near the fruit trees. Songbirds inhabit the pole-sized hardwoods along the upper edge of the field. The pasture itself produces wildflowers in the spring, which attract insects for hungry thrushes, swallows, and eastern bluebirds. The best time to visit is early morning or just before sunset, late spring through early summer.

Directions: Drive approximately four miles north on Route 12 from Woodstock and park at the Appalachian Trail parking area on the left side of the road. Cross the road and hike one mile east on the A.T. to the open area just beneath the summit of Dana Hill.

Closest Town: Woodstock   **Size:** 10 acres

Ownership: USFS, 767-4261; managed and maintained in cooperation with the Dartmouth Outing Club and the Appalachian Trail Conference.

13. APPALACHIAN TRAIL: GIFFORD WOODS STATE PARK

Description: Located on the Appalachian Trail and easily accessed from the town of Sherburne Center, Gifford Woods State Park provides an outstanding example of a northern hardwood forest rich in old growth trees.

Viewing Information: The tall, stratified canopy provides a variety of habitats for songbirds and forest mammals, including white-tailed deer. A leisurely stroll eastward along the Appalachian Trail leads to Kent Pond, where waterfowl and aquatic life may be found. Visit early mornings or just before sunset during late spring and early summer.

Directions: Drive north from Sherburne Center on Routes 4/100. When the road diverges, follow Rt. 100 for 0.5 mile north. Parking for Gifford Woods State Park is on the left.

Closest Town: Sherburne Center   **Size:** 114 acres

Ownership: VTFPR (775-5354); the Appalachian Trail is maintained by the Green Mountain Club and the Appalachian Trail Conference.

14. LEFFERT'S POND

Description: Leffert's Pond is a quiet oasis in a circle of wooded slopes. Open water, marshy edges, and shallow coves make this an ideal site for canoeing. Waterfowl may be seen on the pond, while great blue herons and other wading birds forage along the shore.

Viewing Information: The pond's marshy fringes are ideal habitat for waterfowl and wading birds, best seen in spring and fall—look for the great blue heron, pied-billed grebe, wood duck, and hooded merganser. Common loon and osprey are occasionally sighted. Beaver, river otter, and white-tailed deer are frequently seen; moose are occasional visitors, particularly in spring and summer. Best viewing times are generally mornings and late afternoons.

Directions: *From Rutland, follow Route 4 east for 3 miles to Meadow Lake Drive. Turn left and travel 1.8 miles to Chittenden Dam Road. Turn right and travel 2.8 miles and bear right onto Dam Road. Follow 1.4 miles to Wildcat Road. Turn right and travel 1 mile to first left (dirt road); road will be gated. Continue 0.5 mile to parking area.*

Closest Town: Mendon   **Ownership:** CVPS 773-2711   **Size:** 62 acres

Thriving today, Vermont's white-tailed deer population was nearly extirpated prior to 1800. In 1779, Vermont as an independent territory posted the nation's first closed season on deer hunting. In 1878, deer were introduced from neighboring New York.
STEVE FACCIO

15. PEAVINE

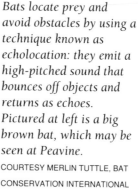

Description: The waters of the White River attract large numbers of flying insects, which in turn draw bats. Nearby is an abandoned talc mine, now the hibernaculum of nearly one thousand bats, including the eastern small-footed bat, a state-listed endangered species.

Viewing Information: A recreation area along the river offers interpretive signs and access to the White River. Atlantic salmon fry are released here in early summer and habitat restoration work has been done by the U.S. Forest Service. Visit a small pull-off located 0.3 mile north of the parking lot on the left side: from here, bats may be seen in large numbers feeding on flying insects during late autumn afternoons and evenings. They are the only major predators of night-flying insects; one bat may consume up to 3,000 insects in a single night.

Directions: *Follow Routes 100/107 north from Stockbridge. Bear left onto Rt. 100 north as the routes divide. Follow 0.8 mile and turn north immediately onto dirt road before steel bridge. Continue 0.6 mile to parking area.*

Closest Town: Stockbridge

Ownership: USFS 767-4261

Size: 50 acres

Bats locate prey and avoid obstacles by using a technique known as echolocation: they emit a high-pitched sound that bounces off objects and returns as echoes. Pictured at left is a big brown bat, which may be seen at Peavine.

COURTESY MERLIN TUTTLE, BAT CONSERVATION INTERNATIONAL

Description: White River is the primary federal facility producing juvenile Atlantic salmon for restoration in the Connecticut River. Approximately 10 million Atlantic salmon eggs are in incubation from October to June, with about 2,000 adult brood fish on station. Visitors may observe salmon up to 30 inches long and weighing 7-10 pounds. The fry are released into selected nursery habitat in several Connecticut River tributaries, where they will leave for the ocean after two years of stream residence. Once they mature and return to their spawning waters in the Connecticut River, these fish will function as the source of future wild Atlantic salmon.

Viewing Information: Visitor center displays interpret the natural life cycle of Atlantic salmon, the hatchery life cycle, and a history of fish hatcheries in the salmon program. Raceways, inside and out, are open to public viewing. *HATCHERY IS CURRENTLY UNDERGOING MAJOR CHANGES IN ITS PRODUCTION PROGRAM AND WILL HAVE MINIMAL FISH VIEWING UNTIL SPRING OF 1995.*

Directions: *From Interstate 89/exit 3, turn right onto Route 107 and travel west to Bethel. Route 107 will make a sharp left and pass under a railroad bridge. Continue 2 miles to hatchery entrance on right.*

Closest Town: Bethel

Ownership: USFWS 234-5241   **Size:** NA

This Atlantic salmon parr will eventually swim its way back into a tributary of the Connecticut River to spawn as an adult. Adult salmon weighing more than twelve pounds may leap ten to twelve feet out of the water. U.S. FISH & WILDLIFE SERVICE

REGION TWO: CENTRAL

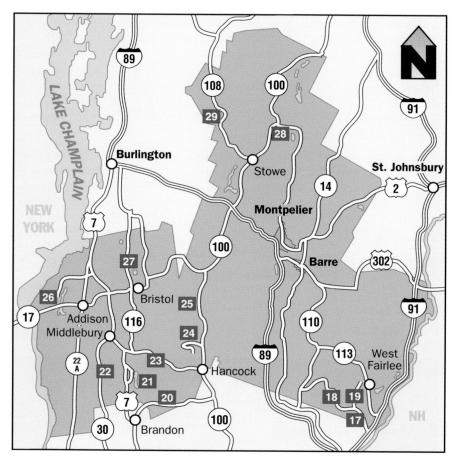

WILDLIFE VIEWING SITES
17. Union Village Mystery Trail
18. Podunk Wildlife Management Area
19. Miller Pond
20. Mount Horrid
21. Blueberry Hill Management Area
22. Cornwall Swamp Wildlife Management Area
23. Robert Frost Interpretive Trail
24. West Hill
25. Granville Gulf Reservation
26. Dead Creek Wildlife Management Area
27. Winona Lake (Bristol Pond)
28. Lamoille County Nature Center
29. Smugglers Notch State Park

17. UNION VILLAGE MYSTERY TRAIL

Description: Beginning at a huge flood-control dam, the setting improves dramatically as visitors continue across the dam and wind their way into a marvelous interior of sedge marsh, river bed, and forest. A natural/cultural history trail explores fields along roads over 200 years old, and leads to a beaver pond.

Viewing Information: An excellent site to look for otters, along with wood duck, hooded merganser, mallard, white-tailed deer, moose, muskrat, beaver, swallow, great blue and green heron, belted kingfisher, and red-tailed hawk. Osprey are also here, an indication that the fishing must be good. Red fox and coyote den in the area. Look for porcupine sign, especially in winter, around the base of hemlocks—porcupine will often be seen up high, gnawing on a limb. *POISON IVY IN SUMMER AND FALL.* A nuisance for people, this plant is a fairly important food source for such species as the ruffed grouse, northern flicker, and cottontail rabbit.

Directions: *Exit Interstate 91 at exit 13, follow Route 5 north to Rt. 132. Follow Rt. 132 for 2 miles to Union Village. Continue to intersection with covered bridge and bear left before bridge. Continue through project entrance, drive over dam. Trailhead is located at third picnic site.*

Closest Town: Thetford Center

Ownership: ACE 649-1606

Size: 975 acres

CENTRAL

The largest member of the weasel family in Vermont, the river otter may weigh up to twenty-five pounds and measure four feet in length. While most of their time is spent in water, otters are capable of traveling overland for great distances between bodies of water. In winter they develop a layer of fat similar to a seal.

STEVE FACCIO

18. PODUNK WILDLIFE MANAGEMENT AREA

Description: Podunk's diverse habitat features a pond, old fields, a deer wintering area, and hardwood forests. Hiking here is strenuous, and rewarding. The left fork of the gated road leads to Podunk pond, while the right follows a feeder stream to a stand of oak and maple trees.

Viewing Information: Look for a variety of woodland and aquatic animal signs. Old apple orchards entice white-tailed deer and black bear, while the beech and oak trees provide good food source for wild turkeys. Porcupines are attracted to hemlocks, particularly in winter. *A HIGH-CLEARANCE FOUR-WHEEL-DRIVE VEHICLE IS NEEDED TO TRAVEL ROADS.*

Directions: *From Route 113 in West Fairlee, turn west onto Beanville Road and travel 0.8 mile. Turn left onto Miller Pond Road, and follow 4.6 miles. Bear right at T-intersection. Travel 0.1 mile to a big stand of maples and stone wall. Pull-offs for parking.*

Closest Town: West Fairlee, Strafford

Ownership: VTFW 479-3241

Size: 924 acres

19. MILLER POND

Description: Thick northern hardwoods and conifers encircle this pond, giving way to sedge and cattails at the shoreline. A Vermont Fish and Wildlife fishing access provides the only point of entry. An angler's trail leads around the water's edge, making for a nice walk.

Viewing Information: This is a good place to visit during migration periods. Listen for spring peepers in early spring. Look for signs of beaver, muskrat, and river otter activity year-round along the water's edge. Belted kingfishers feed on trout and bass while the water is free of ice. Look for the chestnut-sided warbler, American redstart, eastern meadowlark, bobolink, killdeer, and sandpiper. Wood duck and hooded merganser are also present.

Directions: *From downtown West Fairlee on Route 113, turn west onto Beanville Road and travel 0.8 mile to Miller Pond Road. Turn left and continue 2.1 miles to Vermont Fish and Wildlife access on right.*

Closest Town: Fairlee, Strafford

Ownership: VTFW 479-3241

Size: 63 acres

20. MOUNT HORRID

Description: The steep, rocky cliffs of Mount Horrid have long provided nesting sites for peregrine falcons. Extripated in the 1950s, these federally-listed endangered birds were reintroduced in the 1980s. The falcons are best seen from the parking area; also visible from this spot is an active beaver pond.

Viewing Information: Common ravens are often seen here. Falcons and beavers are best viewed from April through August, from the parking area. Watch for cedar waxwings and tree swallows feeding on mosquitoes around the beaver pond, with falcons soaring over the cliffs in the early and late hours of the day; falcons prey on waxwings, as well as other birds, from mid-air. Beaver are seldom seen in daytime; look for signs of their activities, such as chewed branches and downed saplings. Moose are seen occasionally near the pond and along all of Route 73; drivers should be alert for animals near the road, spring through fall, in early morning and at night. *TRAIL TO CLIFF FACE IS CLOSED IN SPRING AND SUMMER TO PROTECT NESTING FALCONS.*

Directions: *From Rochester, travel 0.3 mile south on Route 100. Turn west onto Rt. 73 and continue for 9.7 miles. Parking lot/pull-off is on north side.*

Closest Town: Rochester

Ownership: USFS 767-4777   **Size:** 120 acres

CENTRAL

Its numbers decimated by the pesticide DDT following World War II, the peregrine falcon is successfully making a comeback. Capable of reaching speeds up to 200 miles per hour, this falcon attacks its prey from the air. Several hiking trails in Vermont are closed in spring and summer to protect nesting falcons. STEVE FACCIO

Passenger
pigeon:
extinct 1914

Peregrine
falcon

Osprey

Wood duck

VERMONT'S
NATURAL HERITAGE

Vermont's diverse forests, fields, and wetlands provide homes for many plants and animals. Human activities, past and present, have altered the land, and, in the process, altered wildlife populations as well. Much of Vermont's forested areas were cleared for timber, farming, and grazing. Rivers and streams were dammed. Many species declined.

Huge flights of the passenger pigeon once darkened Vermont's skies. People failed to realize that seemingly abundant wildlife can still be fragile—and the passenger pigeon was lost to extinction. Today the common loon is far from common in Vermont, but wildlife agencies are working to protect nesting habitat.

Today, endangered wildlife such as the peregrine falcon, osprey, and Atlantic salmon are making a comeback in Vermont.

Pine marten

Wild turkey

Common loon

Beaver

Atlantic salmon

21. BLUEBERRY HILL MANAGEMENT AREA

Description: Blueberry Hill is located on the southern end of Hogback Mountain. The lowbush blueberry, a native shrub, grows under the canopy of forested stands in this area. Many years ago, the forested stands were removed for farming. As farms were abandoned, blueberries reclaimed this open meadow. Berries are now maintained by prescribed burning during the spring to remove competing vegetation and to stimulate new growth.

Viewing Information: This site is frequently visited by black bears in late summer during raspberry and blueberry season. The upland attracts a variety of songbirds, including eastern bluebird, indigo bunting, and chestnut-sided warbler. The American kestrel and white-tailed deer are also present.

Directions: From Brandon, travel east on Route 73 for 4.5 miles. Turn north onto Forest Road 32, drive 0.2 mile, and bear left across bridge. Continue 0.2 mile and turn east at 4-way intersection. Turn left on FR 224 to viewing site.

Closest Town: Goshen

Ownership: USFS 388-4362   **Size:** 20 acres

22. CORNWALL SWAMP WILDLIFE MANAGEMENT AREA

Description: This floodplain swamp along Otter Creek is one of the largest wetlands in the Champlain Valley. Bottomland hardwoods, such as northern white cedar, red maple, and green ash, dominate this swamp forest. A major deer wintering area, precaution should be taken not to disturb the western edge during the winter months.

Viewing Information: This habitat is used extensively by white-tailed deer, cottontail rabbit, raccoon, wild turkey, American woodcock, and ruffed grouse. Look for several species of waterfowl: mallard, American black duck, wood duck, and blue- and green-winged teal. Songbirds include the black-throated green warbler, solitary vireo, and hermit thrush. Reptile and amphibians include the northern ringneck snake, midland painted turtle, wood turtle, pickerel frog, northern two-lined salamander, and spotted salamander. *MOSQUITOS THICK IN SUMMER.*

Directions: From Middlebury, travel Route 30 south for 6 miles. Turn east onto Swamp Road and travel 1.4 miles to parking area just before covered bridge.

Closest Town: Cornwall

Ownership: VTFW 878-1564

Size: 1,375 acres

CENTRAL

23. ROBERT FROST INTERPRETIVE TRAIL

Description: Robert Frost spent his last 24 summers near this area. Many of his poems were inspired by time spent in the Green Mountains, where he was also involved in the clearing of several trails. This namesake trail offers a half-hour walk in the Green Mountain National Forest. Interpretive signs identify trees, plants, wildflowers, mountain peaks and land management practices, all cleverly entwined with poems by Frost. A boardwalk leads across a beaver pond, stream, and through a wetland. The trail then passes through an upland forest and into a meadow of blueberries, maintained by prescribed burning.

Viewing Information: This site is actively managed for speckled alder, a small shrub that provides prime habitat for the American woodcock. Black bears visit occasionally in late summer during raspberry and blueberry season. The wetlands attract a variety of songbirds and mammals, such as white-tailed deer, beaver, river otter, mink, wood duck, alder flycatcher, and yellow warbler. Look for red-spotted newt, painted turtle, and common garter and brown snake. Moose are seen occasionally in the early morning and late evening, spring through fall.

Directions: *Travel Route 7 south from Middlebury for 4 miles. Turn east onto Rt. 125 and continue for 4.9 miles. Trail is on south side, a picnic area on north side.*

Closest Town: Ripton

Ownership: USFS 388-4362

Size: 20 acres

Black bears hibernate six to seven months of the year. During this time, they sleep in a shallow state of drowsiness without eating, drinking, urinating, or defecating. Females will, give birth during denning to cubs weighing seven to twelve ounces.
CINDY KILGORE BROWN

24. WEST HILL

Description: This huge parcel of land accommodates a diversity of wildlife. A good example of land management practices by the USDA Forest Service, with interpretive signs along the roadway explaining the stages of timber harvests.

Viewing Information: The apple orchards and abundant berries provide prime black bear and white-tailed deer habitat. Look for signs of moose along trails. Porcupines find plenty of food in this woody area, as do ruffed grouse and American woodcock. Listen for the calls of owls and coyotes at night in summer and fall, and the drumming of ruffed grouse in early spring. Ladyslippers and trilliums may be seen in damp, shady areas in April and May.

Directions: Follow Route 100 north of Granville for 0.2 mile. Turn left in the sharp curve just after passing the Vermont Only Village Store. Follow Forest Road 55 along the stream to a parking area, or continue along FR 55 or FR 101.

Closest Town: Granville

Ownership: USFS 767-4261

Size: 1,500 acres

25. GRANVILLE GULF RESERVATION

Description: *AUTO TOUR.* This 6-mile auto route weaves through a series of wetlands, a stand of tall pines, and passes an impressive waterfall, Moss Glen Falls. The headwaters of both the White River (running south) and the Mad River (running north) are found in the gulf area.

Viewing Information: A good area to observe white-tailed deer and moose during spring, summer, and fall as they cross Route 100 frequently in the early morning and again in the evening. Beaver ponds are generally active from spring until late fall. Migrating and nesting waterfowl can be seen in early spring, with red-tailed hawk, belted kingfisher, and great blue heron seen often around the wetlands.

Directions: Follow Route 100 North of Granville for 1.2 miles. Travel 1.5 miles to Moss Glen Falls, and continue for another 1.5 miles through a series of wetlands, forest edge, and the stand of pines where moose frequently cross.

Closest Town: Granville

Ownership: VTFPR 483-2314

Size: Six-mile drive; 1,171 acres

26. DEAD CREEK WILDLIFE MANAGEMENT AREA

Description: Dead Creek's open meadow, marsh, and open waterways make for excellent canoeing with a high probability of seeing a variety of wetlands wildlife. The area was originally managed to provide a nesting and migratory resting and feeding area for Canada geese. Through the years, it has become a major stopover for snow geese on their southerly migration. During years of impoundment drainage, Dead Creek attracts thousands of migrating shorebirds between July and September. This site offers scenic views of Camel's Hump to the east and the Adirondack Mountains to the west in New York.

Viewing Information: October is a magical month for viewing, as thousands of migrating Canada and snow geese rest and feed in and around the refuge; geese and other birds are easily observed by vehicle from the designated parking areas. During the fall, the best time for viewing geese in flight is from daylight to 8:30 a.m., and near dusk. Geese rest during mid-day. A portion of this refuge is a popular waterfowl hunting area during the fall. Throughout the year, this site offers good sightings of wild turkey, great horned and common screech owl, northern harrier, red-tailed hawk, American kestrel, and other hawks. *ENTRY ONTO REFUGE GROUNDS IS PROHIBITED. SPRING CANOEING IS DISCOURAGED DUE TO NESTING WATERFOWL.*

Directions: *From Route 22A in Addison, turn west on Route 17. From this point, watch fields on either side of the road for geese. Four access areas are marked along road.*

Closest Town: Addison

Ownership: VTFW 759-2398   **Size:** 2,858 acres

Snow geese usually migrate at altitudes above 2,000 feet, flying in wavy lines rather than in the familiar V-formation attributed to Canada geese. Passing through Vermont, they will winter as far south as North Carolina before returning to their breeding grounds in the eastern Arctic.
CINDY KILGORE BROWN

27. WINONA LAKE (BRISTOL POND)

Description: Nestled beneath Hogback Mountain, Bristol Pond can best be enjoyed by canoeists, though it is also accessible through binoculars or a spotting scope. Cattails and heath surround the edges, with a brook feeding the pond.

Viewing Information: From the shoreline an osprey's nest can be seen to the south atop a tall dead tree. Great blue herons fish among the shoreline reeds. The common merganser and wood duck are summer residents, along with belted kingfisher, American kestrel, common raven, water snake, muskrat, and butterfly species. Autumn brings migrating waterfowl—the area is popular with waterfowl hunters at this time. The pond supports a healthy population of largemouth bass, northern pike, bluegill, pickerel, bullhead, and yellow perch.

Directions: *From Bristol, travel west on Route 17. At the main intersection in town, turn north on North Street and follow 3.1 miles to Vermont Fish and Wildlife access area on the right.*

Closest Town: Bristol

Ownership: VTFW 878-1564

Size: 234 acres

28. LAMOILLE COUNTY NATURE CENTER

Description: This site is an outdoor teaching area for a local nonprofit environmental organization. Attractions include two nature trails, a council-sized Sioux tepee, an outdoor amphitheater, and a "Streamco" willow plantation, used throughout New England for streambank restoration programs. The nature trails, both self-guided and free to the public, explore the diverse habitat of northern deciduous and boreal forest. Call for program information.

Viewing Information: Walking the trails, look for signs of white-tailed deer, black bear, yellow-bellied sapsucker, and pileated woodpecker. Songbirds include hermit thrush, evening grosbeak, and red-breasted nuthatch. Ladyslippers bloom in early summer.

Directions: *From Stowe, travel Route 100N for approximately 2 miles. Turn left onto Stagecoach Road. At Morristown, 4-corners, take a left onto Walton Road. Turn left onto Cole Hill Road and continue less than 1 mile to parking on the right.*

Closest Town: Morrisville

Ownership: Lamoille County Natural Resources Conservation District
888-4965

Size: 40 acres

29. SMUGGLERS NOTCH STATE PARK

Description: Once the route of smugglers transporting liquor and other goods over the Canada - U.S. border during prohibition, this site is located on a gap between Sterling Peak and Mount Mansfield, Vermont's tallest peak at 4,393 feet. The Long Trail crosses the Notch and several trails lead to both summits. This area supports the only extensive alpine tundra in Vermont. The summit may be reached by toll road, gondola, or by hiking the Cliff or Long Trail. A historic nesting site for peregrine falcons—the birds use the area for roosting and nesting today.

Viewing Information: Look for signs of black bear in late summer around the higher elevations, where blueberries grow. Coyote and fisher are known inhabitants of the larger forested areas. The summits provide a good area to view hawk migrations in the fall. Listen for white-throated sparrow, junco, and black-poll warbler. Comon raven is a year-round resident and nests on the Notch. Watch for snow bunting during fall in the alpine regions. Hiking is discouraged in April/May as wet conditions from melting snow and foot travel cause erosion. Ranger-naturalists patrol the Notch during the summer to educate the public about this unique environment. *EXTREMELY FRAGILE PLANT LIFE—STAY ON TRAILS WHEN HIKING.*

Directions: *From the intersection of Routes 100 and 108 in Stowe, travel Rt. 108 North for 6.2 miles to the Notch Passageway. Continue another 3 miles to State Ski Dorm and Hostel and Smugglers Notch State Park.*

Closest Town: Stowe   **Ownership:** VTFPR 253-4014   **Size:** 4,000 Acres

Due in part to birdfeeders, the evening grosbeak has become more prevalent in Vermont over the past few years. Formerly this stocky finch bred no farther east than Minnesota.

RICHARD PILIERO

REGION THREE: NORTHEAST KINGDOM

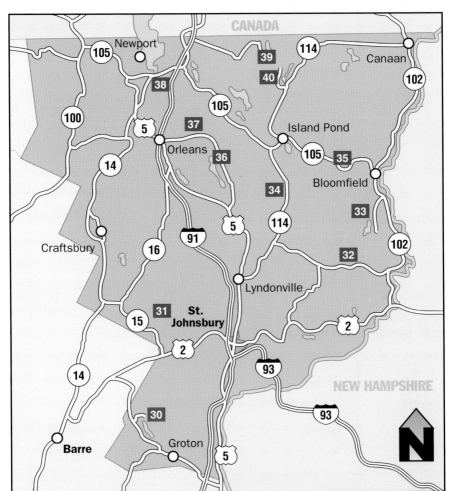

WILDLIFE VIEWING SITES
30. Groton State Forest
31. Steam Mill Brook Wildlife Management Area
32. Victory Basin Wildlife Management Area
33. Maidstone State Park
34. Route 114
35. Wenlock Wildlife Management Area
36. Mount Pisgah
37. Willoughby Falls, Willoughby Falls Wildlife Management Area
38. South Bay Wildlife Management Area
39. Bill Sladyk Wildlife Management Area: Holland Pond Access
40. Bill Sladyk Wildlife Management Area: Route 114 Access

41

30. GROTON STATE FOREST

Description: Vermont's largest state-owned forest is rich with habitat, ranging from lakes, ponds, bogs, and mountains to hills and meadows. Many points of interest are linked by an extensive trail system; maps may be obtained at the nature center. Gated roads may be hiked. *BE ALERT FOR LOGGING TRUCKS, WHICH HAVE RIGHT-OF-WAY.*

Viewing Information: Sixteen species of warbler have been sighted here. Area waters provide food and shelter for migrating and nesting waterfowl, as well as river otter, mink, and beaver. Black bear scat may be seen on logging roads around apple orchards in late summer and early fall. Around Peacham and Osmore ponds, look for beaver hutches and signs of white-tailed deer and moose. Common loons may be seen or heard at Lake Groton. Owl's Head is an excellent place for viewing migrating hawks in late summer and early fall; watch for ruffed grouse, red-breasted nuthatch, yellow-bellied sapsucker, and scarlet tanager along this knoll as well.

Directions: From Barre, follow Route 302 east for 15 miles. Turn northwest onto Rt. 232 and travel 2 miles to Boulder Beach Recreation Area, 6.4 miles to Owl's Head parking area, and 7 miles to New Discovery Recreation Area.

Closest Town: Groton   **Ownership:** VTFPR 584-3823   **Size:** 25,625 acres

Like other Vermont ponds, Osmore offers migrating waterfowl a resting and feeding area, breeding waters for thousands of amphibians, and fishing opportunities for the belted kingfisher, osprey, hooded merganser, common loon, raccoon, mink, and river otter. MARGARET YOUNG

31. STEAM MILL BROOK WILDLIFE MANAGEMENT AREA

Description: Steam Mill Brook includes a large tract of hardwood forest, spruce-fir forest, and wetlands. The northern hardwoods include beech, birch, and maple stands—good black bear habitat. Balsam fir dominates the softwood stands. At an elevation of approximately 2,200 feet, Coles Pond is easily accessed via automobile; Stannard Pond is a remote, pristine body of water, reached only on foot.

Viewing Information: This large, undeveloped forest tract provides year-round habitat for white-tailed deer and moose. The presence of suitable denning sites, along with blueberries, raspberries, cherries, apples, and beechnuts, make this area especially attractive to bears. Habitat for the snowshoe hare, an important prey species for red fox, coyote, fisher, and bobcat, has improved as a result of forest management practices. Look for signs of river otter, mink, and beaver around wetlands, along with upland birds, including the ruffed grouse and American woodcock. Stannard Pond and its tributaries support brook trout. Gates have been installed here to preserve a hike-in "wilderness" experience, and to protect bears.

Directions: At the intersection of Routes 2 and 15, follow Rt. 15 west for 3 miles. In the sharp curve, continue straight onto dirt road. Follow for 0.8 mile to first right, which continues 1.6 miles to uplands parking area of WMA; or drive an additional 3.8 miles to Coles Pond turn. Turn right, follow 0.6 mile, bear right again and continue 2 miles to WMA parking access at pond.

Closest Town: West Danville, Hardwick

Ownership: VTFW 748-8787

Size: 8,440 acres

While appearing gawky to the human eye, a moose weighing up to 1,400 pounds may reach speeds of thirty-five miles per hour. Moose can also swim eight to twelve miles and dive to depths of eighteen feet.
CINDY KILGORE BROWN

32. VICTORY BASIN WILDLIFE MANAGEMENT AREA

Description: Through every season, from every angle, Victory Basin offers stunning scenic views of a remote northern ecosystem. The habitats include lowland spruce-fir forests, upland hardwoods, sedge meadows, alder swales, river, and bog. Five miles of hiking trails and many gated logging roads can be explored on foot. Experienced canoeists may get optimal viewing along Bog Brook and the Moose River. There are three parking areas within the 8.9 miles of road frontage of this WMA.

Viewing Information: This is black bear country during berry season in late July and August. Red fox travel along the forest edge. Look for signs of pileated woodpeckers in the ragged cavities of dead trees. American bittern easily blends into the reedy cover of the water's edge. This site is also home to moose, white-tailed deer, raccoon, fisher, river otter, American woodcock, ruffed grouse, common snipe, barred, great horned and saw-whet owl, rusty blackbird, and snapping turtle.

Directions: Follow Route 2 to North Concord, take a left onto Victory Road and travel 4 miles. The road is well-maintained gravel between the villages of Victory and Gallup Mills. Look for Wildlife Management Area signs and parking areas.

Closest Town: Victory

Ownership: VTFW 748-8787

Size: 4,970 acres

The red fox has the largest geographical range of any carnivore worldwide.
STEVE FACCIO

44

33. MAIDSTONE STATE PARK

Description: This site lies near the Maidstone State Forest and includes remote ponds and streams on undeveloped forest lands. The most significant feature here is picturesque Maidstone Lake, of glacial origin. Only one-third of the shoreline is state-owned, the remainder in private hands. Day-use facilities are set within a mature stand of spruce and fir forest, while the campground lies within a mixed northern hardwood forest. A variety of wildlife exists here, including white-tailed deer, black bear, moose, and river otter.

Viewing Information: Several hiking trails venture alongside the lake and through spruce and fir stands. Look and listen for songbirds such as hermit thrush, red-breasted nuthatch, and evening grosbeak. Look for signs of porcupine—these mammals prefer the bark of conifers and hardwoods. Moose, white-tailed deer, snowshoe hare, and fisher may also be detected in this habitat. The hardwood forest supports ruffed grouse, chipmunks, and squirrels; predators such as great horned and barred owl, broad-winged hawk, northern goshawk, coyote, and red fox are also present. Woodpeckers feed and nest in standing dead trees. Common loons may be seen or heard on the lake. Trillium, bloodroot, and Jack-in-the-pulpit bloom in spring.

Directions: *From the junction of Route 105 and Rt. 102 in Bloomfield, follow Rt. 102 south for 4.2 miles. Turn west and follow 3.8 miles to park entrance.*

Closest Town: Bloomfield   **Ownership:** VTFPR 676-3930   **Size:** 471 acres

34. ROUTE 114

Description: *AUTO TOUR.* Route 114 from East Burke to Canaan is a 20-mile route continuously flanked with "licks," areas where salt used on winter roads runs off and accumulates in bogs. Moose are attracted to these areas in spring and summer, adding this nutrient to their diet after a winter of woody browse. *NO FACILITIES ALONG THIS ROUTE.*

Viewing Information: Drive this route scannining bogs on roadsides for tracks, stop in pull-offs along the road. Best viewing is after a rain, when salt-rich water recharges the licks. Find one with fresh tracks, and wait patiently. Best viewing between 5:30 a.m. and 9:30 a.m., and again at dusk. *BEWARE OF MOOSE ENTERING ROAD, AND BE ALERT FOR TRAFFIC, INCLUDING LOGGING TRUCKS IN EARLY MORNING.*

Directions: *Follow Route 114 north of East Burke.*

Closest Town: East Burke, Island Pond, Canaan

Ownership: NA   **Size:** A 20-mile stretch of Route 114

Description: Wenlock is part of the largest deer wintering area in the state. During winter months, deer concentrate here for shelter from deep snows and cold winds. Additional stress to wintering deer caused by human disturbance can be fatal, making it best to avoid this area from mid-December through March. Between spring and autumn, the logging roads may be traveled or hiked. *LOGGING TRUCK TRAFFIC; TRUCKS HAVE RIGHT-OF-WAY.*

Viewing Information: During spring, summer, and fall, moose may be observed along Route 105 in the early morning and again in late afternoon. Look for black bear scat along dirt roads. This southerly range of the boreal forest is home to a number of uncommon species in Vermont, such as the boreal chickadee, gray jay, black-backed three-toed woodpecker, and the endangered spruce grouse.

Directions: *From Island Pond, travel east on Route 105 for 9 miles.*

Closest Town: Island Pond

Ownership: VTFW 748-8787

Size: 1,994 acres

The female spruce grouse nests on the ground and loses her scent during this time, making it difficult for predators like the red fox, striped skunk, and bobcat to find her. To lure predators away from the nest, she will cry out as if wounded, and feign injury, drooping one wing and trailing a leg.
CHARLES WILLEY

Description: Located within the Willoughby State Forest, Mount Pisgah reaches an elevation of 2,751 feet, and drops sharply into Lake Willoughby. This glacial lake is one of New England's deepest, with a depth exceeding 300 feet. Raptors are the attraction here, and the peregrine falcon has top billing. Best viewing is from the north end of the west-facing cliff, which overlooks the lake; views are spectacular in summer and fall. *BEWARE OF SUDDEN WEATHER CHANGES ON MOUNTAIN PEAK.*

Viewing Information: Mount Pisgah is one of the state's historical nesting sites for peregrine falcons. These magnificent birds returned here in 1985, ending a 30-year absence. Watch for returning falcons in spring. Nesting takes place during the summer, and the birds generally leave by August. Look for early morning and late afternoon activity. Watch the sky as peregrines hunt other birds, from above, "stooping" at tremendous speeds to seize them in mid-air. *BINOCULARS OR SPOTTING SCOPE HIGHLY RECOMMENDED.*

Directions: *Exit Interstate 91 north at Barton and travel Route 16 north for 0.8 mile. Turn onto Rt. 5 south and drive 0.2 mile back to Rt. 16 heading east. Follow 5.8 miles to Rt. 5A south. Follow 4.5 miles to parking area on the right.*

Closest Town: Barton

Ownership: VTFPR 748-8787

Size: 130 acres

One of Vermont's most scenic surroundings, Mount Pisgah supports a number of arctic plants along its steep, rocky walls.
CINDY KILGORE BROWN

NORTHEAST KINGDOM

Great horned owl

Striped skunk

PREDATORS AND PREY

Visit a beaver pond on a June day and you may see a brood of wood ducks, a muskrat family, or perhaps a school of minnows.

The serenity of the above scenes, however, is not a constant in nature. Some of the ducklings may succumb to disease. Many of the young muskrats may starve. A few of the young from either family are almost certain to be killed by a snapping turtle, a mink, or another predator.

The relationship between predators and prey is entirely natural. Predators kill other animals in order to eat and stay alive. Yet predators are sometimes reviled by humans because they kill animals considered harmless or defenseless, or more desireable.

Snapping turtle

Wood duck chick

Predator-prey cycle of gray fox & cottontail rabbit   REED A. PRESCOTT III

37. WILLOUGHBY FALLS, WILLOUGHBY FALLS WILDLIFE MANAGEMENT AREA

Description: Witness one of nature's springtime spectacles at Willoughby Falls. Between the last week of April and the second week in May, wild rainbow trout navigate the torrent of the falls, pushing upstream to complete their annual spawning run. From the bridge downstream, or at vantage points on either side of the falls, visitors can marvel as these silver, two-foot-long fish make acrobatic leaps to clear the whitewater.

Viewing Information: The annual "rainbow run" begins in the deep, cold waters of Lake Memphremagog. When trout mature, they return to spawn in the fast water and clean gravel beds of the Willoughby River and its small feeder streams, where they were hatched 2 to 5 years earlier. Their ascent of Willoughby Falls presents a great opportunity for viewing or photography. Leaping activity is not constant and it is impossible to predict which days or times offer the best viewing. Warm afternoons, when water temperatures rise through the 40-degree range, seem to trigger increased movement and jumping.

Directions: *From Orleans, travel east on Route 58 toward Brownington for 0.2 mile. Bear left at the "Brownington" sign and travel 0.1 mile to the Vermont Fish and Wildlife parking area.*

Closest Town: Orleans

Ownership: VTFW 748-8787

Size: 3 acres; 130 acres

When migrating rainbow trout leave the water in a spectacular effort to clear a waterfall, it may appear to be an unproductive struggle. Most of the time, these fish travel underwater along the eddies.
JIM BLAKESLEE

38. SOUTH BAY WILDLIFE MANAGEMENT AREA

Description: The marsh on the edge of the shoreline is the real appeal here. Pickerelweed, rushes, cattails, and sedges provide cover, food, and nesting habitat for many wildlife species. While it can be enjoyed from the fishing access with binoculars, it is best experienced by canoe or electric motor boat.

Viewing Information: This is a site for an occasional bald eagle, also historic osprey nesting area. Great blue and green heron, and American bittern. A large colony of black terns nests here. Painted and snapping turtle are residents. This is the most important waterfowl migration area in northeastern Vermont. Best viewing between late summer and autumn. *AVOID EARLY SUMMER VISITS TO PROTECT NESTING WATERFOWL.*

Directions: *Travel Interstate 91 north to exit 27 and follow Route 191 west to Rt. 5 south. Cross the bridge between South Bay and Lake Memphremagog, turn left at Coventry Street and continue about 0.5 mile to Vermont Fish and Wildlife access.*

Closest Town: Newport

Ownership: VTFW 748-8787

Size: 1,559 acres

Known more as a coastal bird, the black tern breeds on inland freshwater lakes and wetlands. They nest in colonies which are often seen on top of muskrat and beaver lodges, as they prefer to be elevated and surrounded by water.
STEVE FACCIO

39. BILL SLADYK WILDLIFE MANAGEMENT AREA: HOLLAND POND ACCESS

Description: This is big country—be sure to bring a compass if exploring the many trails. Beaver and Round ponds are stocked with brook trout and may be accessed by canoe from Holland Pond. The haunting call of the common loon may be heard from early spring until late fall. There are several private roads off Holland Pond; please respect landowners' rights and don't trespass.

Viewing Information: The ponds' healthy brook and rainbow trout populations attract many fish-eating species, such as osprey, common loon, belted kingfisher, river otter, and mink. The southern end of the pond is quite marshy, with alders, sphagnum, and grass-covered tussocks. As the ice thaws, frogs, toads, and salamanders breed in the marshes; wading birds, such as the great blue heron, along with raccoon, mink, and river otter, dine on the amphibians. *THIS AREA MAY BE POSTED MAY THROUGH JULY TO PROTECT NESTING LOONS.* In the northern section of Holland Pond, look for moose and their trails leading from Holland to Turtle Pond. In winter, designated trails are kept open by local snowmobile clubs—these may be snowshoed or skied. *SNOWMOBILES HAVE RIGHT-OF-WAY. STAY ON TRAILS AND AVOID AREAS USED BY WINTERING DEER.*

Directions: *From Morgan on Route 111, turn north onto paved road beside Seymour Lake Lodge. Follow 4.7 miles and bear right onto dirt road. Continue 5.3 miles to pond parking area.*

Closest Town: Morgan

Ownership: VTFW 748-8787

Size: 210 acres (pond)

NORTHEAST KINGDOM

The cry of the common loon can signal excitation, stress, and distress in four basic calls: the wail, yodel, tremolo, and hoot. Loons are extremely sensitive to the presence of people—enjoy these birds from a distance.
CHARLES WILLEY

40. BILL SLADYK WILDLIFE MANAGEMENT AREA: RT. 114 ACCESS

Description: This site borders Quebec and is the state's largest WMA. The terrain is flat to rolling hills, very typical of the Northeast Kingdom. Access includes Hurricane Brook, Cranberry Bog, and portions of Norton Pond, as well as forested upland areas. Approximately 6 miles of roads may be traveled, and more than 40 miles of trails. Roads are not maintained in winter, but may be traveled via snowshoe, cross-country skis, or snowmobile.

Viewing Information: Virtually all of this site is forested. Northern hardwoods are found along the ridges, with spruce-fir stands along stream bottoms and swamp areas. Look for signs of white-tailed deer, moose, and black bear. Boreal bird species include Canada jay, black-backed three-toed woodpecker, boreal chickadee, and common loon. Ruffed grouse may be detected in the brushy cover of recently-cut hardwoods. American woodcock may be seen or heard along forest edges. Young softwood stands provide good habitat for snowshoe hare and its predators, such as coyote, red fox, fisher, and bobcat. Streams and ponds support mink, river otter, beaver, and muskrat.

Directions: *Follow Route 114 north from Island Pond for 5.6 miles to Hurricane Brook Road on left. Follow 0.1 mile into WMA.*

Closest Town: Island Pond   **Ownership:** VTFW 748-8787

Size: 9,385 acres

During spring courtship, the male ruffed grouse will cup his wings and bring them forcefully forward, making a low drumming sound that will carry half a mile. Drumming invites females to join him, and warns males of his territory.
STEVE FACCIO

REGION FOUR: NORTHWEST LAKE

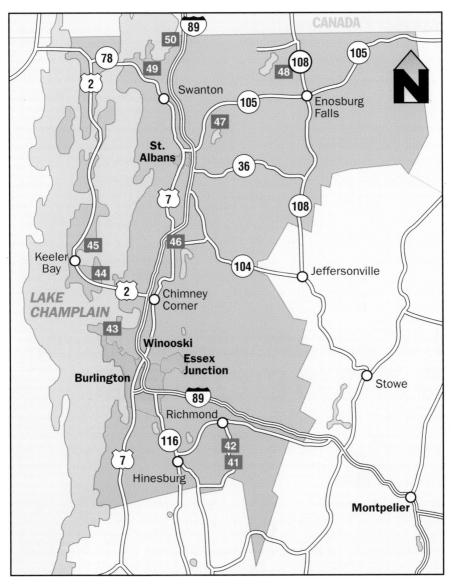

WILDLIFE VIEWING SITES
41. The Birds of Vermont Museum
42. Green Mountain Audubon Nature Center
43. Malletts Bay State Park
44. Sand Bar Wildlife Management Area
45. Ed Weed Fish Culture Station
46. Arrowhead Mountain Lake
47. Fairfield Swamp Wildlife Management Area
48. Lake Carmi State Park
49. Missiquoi National Wildlife Refuge
50. Shad Island and Bird's Foot Delta

41. THE BIRDS OF VERMONT MUSEUM

Description: Established to exhibit and preserve the woodcarvings of Robert N. Spear, Jr., this museum also interprets Vermont's bird species. Open daily May 1 through October 31 (except Tuesdays), from 10:00 a.m. to 4:00 p.m.

Viewing Information: More than 170 bird exhibits, each displaying a male and female of the species, their nest and eggs, and a habitat sample. Dioramas interpret another 73 species. A one-way glass window looks out upon a bird sanctuary, with its sounds piped in. The bird feeders hosts hummingbirds, evening and rose-breasted grosbeak, woodpeckers, and American goldfinch. Nesting species include eastern bluebird and American woodcock.

Directions: *Take exit 11 off Interstate 89. At stoplight in Richmond, turn right towards Huntington and continue to Sherman Hollow Road.*

Closest Town: Richmond

Ownership: Nonprofit organization 434-2167

Size: NA

42. GREEN MOUNTAIN AUDUBON NATURE CENTER

Description: This facility offers 300 acres of varied habitats, including decidious and coniferous forest, marsh, swamp, beaver ponds, meadow, stream, and the Huntington River. Five miles of trails are maintained and open free of charge every day from dawn to dusk. Interpretive materials are available in the visitor center.

Viewing Information: The varied habitat offers opportunities to chance upon great blue heron, beaver, mink, wood duck, white-tailed deer, rabbit, red fox, moose, as well as hummingbirds, owls, and 64 songbird species. A variety of creative programs include nature walks and workshops, school tours, and seasonal celebrations such as Winter Solstice, Spring Equinox, and Summer Solstice. Admission varies; call for information.

Directions: *Take exit 11 off Interstate 89 and travel west for 2 miles to Richmond. Turn right at stoplight and continue 5 miles, following signs to Huntington.*

Closest Town: Richmond

Ownership: Green Mountain Audubon Society 434-3068

Size: 300 acres

43. MALLETTS BAY STATE PARK

Description: This undeveloped park is located on 200 acres along the north shore of Malletts Bay. A small stream, Trout Brook, divides the property, slicing a ravine deep into the sandy terrace between two wooded limestone ridges. The 4,700 feet of shoreline is similarly divided, with one half a sandy beach into shallow water, and the other a series of spectacular cedar-covered ledges plunging into a rocky cove.

Viewing Information: Beaver activity is obvious along Trout Brook, as is amphibian life—look for map turtles and bullfrogs. Ruffed grouse and cottontail rabbit are common along the terrace, while great blue heron and seasonal waterfowl frequent the shallows off the beach. White-tailed deer have a wintering area within this site. Wild turkey, red fox, raccoon, skunk, snowshoe hare, coyote, fisher, and porcupines are residents. Muskrat, mink, and river otter sign may be found along the water's edge. Look and listen for such raptors as great horned and barred owl, and red-tailed hawk. Trillium, both red and white, bloom along the roadside in late spring.

Directions: *Take exit 17 off Interstate 89, follow Route 2 west for 1 mile to Raymond Road. Approximately 0.25-mile south on Raymond Road is entry to a boulder-lined parking area on left. The half-mile path to the beach follows the narrow service road on the other side of the gate.*

Closest Town: Colchester, Milton

Ownership: VTFPR 879-6565

Size: 200 acres

One of the smallest frogs, spring peepers weigh just one-tenth of an ounce. Their high-pitched chirping may be audible one-half mile away. Females will attach 600 to 1,200 eggs individually to aquatic plants; eggs hatch within a week.
TED LEVIN

NORTHWEST LAKE

44. SAND BAR WILDLIFE MANAGEMENT AREA

Description: This site is located on the edge of Lake Champlain; the marsh-land is of Lamoille River delta origin. The bottomlands are made up of cotton-wood, willow, red maple, and ash. Shrub growth along the channel includes alder, buttonbush, and willow, with emergent vegetation of burreed, cattail, arrowhead, sedges, wild rice, and grasses. An intensive wood duck nesting program has been in progress since 1948. One hundred and fifty nesting boxes with predator shields are monitored here for productivity.

Viewing Information: Good viewing and photographic opportunities within the marshy edges of Lake Champlain. The Vermont Fish and Wildlife access across from Sand Bar State Park provides a good area to view with binoculars or spotting scope. The Lamoille delta may be accessed with canoe, but *RE-SPECT THE REFUGE BOUNDARY SIGNS.* Breeding waterfowl include the wood duck, blue-winged teal, American black duck, mallard, common golden-eye, and hooded merganser. Marsh birds such as great blue heron, Virginia rail, and moorhen frequent the reedy shore. A nesting pair of osprey are present and may be seen fishing over open water. Listen for a variety of owls. Look for signs of beaver, mink, muskrat, and river otter in the wetlands, as well as the upland species of white-tailed deer, wild turkey, ruffed grouse, red fox, coyote, raccoon, porcupine, and striped skunk.

Directions: *Follow Interstate 89 north to exit 17, follow Route 2 east for 8 miles to Sand Bar State Park on right—directly across is Vermont Fish and Wildlife access.*

Closest Town: Milton

Ownership: VTFW 878-1564

Size: 1,660 acres

The male, or drake, wood duck is considered by many the most beautiful duck in North America. Wood ducks nest in tree cavities and may be found around creeks, rivers, flood-plain lakes, swamps, and beaver ponds.

RUSSELL HANSEN

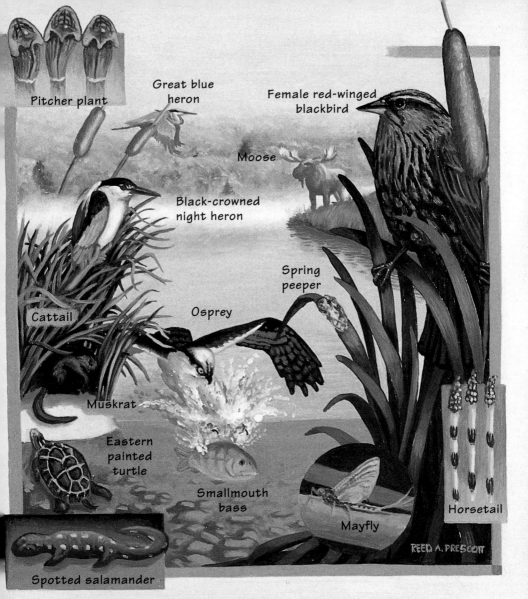

Pitcher plant

Great blue heron

Female red-winged blackbird

Moose

Black-crowned night heron

Cattail

Osprey

Spring peeper

Muskrat

Eastern painted turtle

Smallmouth bass

Mayfly

Horsetail

REED A. PRESCOTT

Spotted salamander

NOT-SO-HIDDEN TREASURE: VERMONT WETLANDS

Vermont's rich assortment of marshes, bogs, swamps, and seasonally-flooded meadows are remnants of the last glacial age. These wetlands have long performed their unique functions of water filtration and flood protection, along with providing essential habitat for many species of fish and wildlife.

Acre for acre, wetlands are some of the most fertile habitats in the world. Many of Vermont's 300,000 acres of wetlands are highly accessible for wildlife viewers, and provide great places to see and photograph animals. Explore from a trail, the roadside, or by canoe. Sites 26, 27, 38, and 47 in this guide are outstanding examples of wetlands, and are well worth a visit.

Perch

Walleye

Bull pout

45. ED WEED FISH CULTURE STATION

Description: Nearly one-half million fish are raised here for distribution throughout the state. Attractions include an elaborate visitor center, a raceway enclosure (larger rearing units), and a walk-through area with displays about fish, fish culture, and aquatic ecosystems. Aquariums display the warm, cold, and cool-water fish species found in Lake Champlain. Hatchery is open daily from 8 a.m. to 4 p.m.; no admission fee.

Viewing Information: View brook, brown, rainbow and lake trout, and land-locked salmon—observation of yearling and juvenile fish can be made at the raceways. Educational displays at visitor center interpret hatchery operations and native aquatic environment. Videos describe fish culture practices and fishing for beginners. A 20-minute self-guided tour (with brochure) offers interpretive and viewing opportunities. Near the lakeshore, waterfowl can be seen year-round, with migrating fish present in fall.

Directions: *Follow Interstate 89 North to exit 17, turn west onto Route 2. Follow for 11 miles passing through South Hero. Turn left onto Rt. 314 and follow 2 miles to hatchery on right.*

Closest Town: Grand Isle

Ownership: VTFW 372-3171

Size: 160 acres

Widely introduced into America in the 19th century, the brown trout is a true trout. From October to December, it moves into feeder streams to spawn. The brown is more tolerant of warm water temperatures and pollution than other species of trout. FREDERICK PRADON

46. ARROWHEAD MOUNTAIN LAKE

Description: This large lake is actually an impoundment of the Lamoille River. While a good portion of the lake can be viewed from Route 7, the most interesting areas lie to the northeast, where the river flows into the lake before emptying into Lake Champlain, several miles to the west by the Sand Bar Wildlife Management Area (see site 44).

Viewing Information: The northeastern section presents a wide, marshy area with islands—excellent habitat for such cavity-nesting waterfowl as wood duck, hooded merganser, and common goldeneye. Look for signs of red-winged blackbird, muskrat, river otter, and mink around the cattails. American bittern, and great blue and green heron fish along the tall reeds. Watch for belted kingfisher and osprey hovering above in search of fish.

Directions: Follow Route 7N past Milton for 4 miles. Turn east on Route 104A and travel 0.9 mile to wetlands on either side of the road. A Vermont Fish and Wildlife fishing access is 0.3 mile farther. Continue an additional 0.5 mile to bridge over the Lamoille River: from here, follow along the wetlands on this quiet road, which also has a small boat access.

Closest Town: Milton

Ownership: CVPS, 773-2711; VTFW (access area), 878-1564

Size: 732 acres

As demonstrated in this photo, the American bittern can go easily unnoticed as it freezes, with bill raised, to blend into the cattails and rushes of its wetlands habitat. In spring, listen for the unusual "oong-KA-chunk" call of this wading bird.
STEVE FACCIO

47. FAIRFIELD SWAMP WILDLIFE MANAGEMENT AREA

Description: This site is half wetlands habitat, with the other half divided between northern hardwoods, swamp hardwoods, and a large stand of northern white cedar. The wetlands habitat produces numerous broods of waterfowl and has about 60 wood duck nesting boxes.

Viewing Information: A good site for canoeing. Look for wood duck and hooded merganser in the wooded swamps. Wetlands provide prime habitat for beaver, river otter, muskrat, raccoon, and bullfrog. Look for ruffed grouse, American woodcock, snowshoe hare, grebes, barred and great horned owl, osprey, and migrating bald and golden eagle. Red and gray fox, coyote, and bobcat are present, though difficult to see. *MOSQUITOES IN SPRING AND EARLY SUMMER.*

Directions: *From St. Albans, travel 7 miles east on Route 36 to parking lot and canoe launch.*

Closest Town: St. Albans

Ownership: VTFW 878-1564

Size: 1,293 acres

48. LAKE CARMI STATE PARK

Description: Located on a 1,375-acre lake with 2 miles of shoreline, this park includes a cattail marsh, stream, meadow, northern hardwood/coniferous forest, and Black Spruce Bog, the third-largest (140-acre) peat bog in the state. Entry fee in summer.

Viewing Information: Lake Carmi provides for a variety of birds: osprey, northern harrier, ruffed grouse, American woodcock, common snipe, bobolink, warblers, grosbeaks, veerys, and great blue and green heron. Signs of river otter, white-tailed deer, and raccoon are seen frequently around wetlands, as are snapping turtle, bullfrog, spring peeper, and garter snake. April through May, listen for the drumming of ruffed grouse. In May and June, view breeding warblers, American woodcock, and common snipe. Early spring brings osprey, merganser, and ring-necked duck.

Directions: *From St. Albans, follow Route 105 east for 15 miles to Rt. 236. Follow Rt. 236 north for 3 miles to park entrance.*

Closest Town: Enosberg Falls

Ownership: VTFPR 933-8383

Size: 482 acres

49. MISSISQUOI NATIONAL WILDLIFE REFUGE

Description: Vermont's only national wildlife refuge, Missisquoi includes woodland and shrub swamps, hayfields and old fields undergoing succession, and forested areas.

Viewing Information: Explore a 1.5-mile nature trail located behind refuge headquarters. June through October offers good viewing of warbler species, bobolink, oriole, woodpeckers, American redstart, hawks, American kestrel, American woodcock, waterfowl, and herons. Watch for white-tailed deer, beaver, muskrat, and river otter. Along the Missisquoi River, great blue heron may be seen any time the water is free of ice. Autumn brings migratory waterfowl, including blue-winged and green-winged teal, pintail, and American wigeon. Nesting birds include northern harrier, American bittern, and common snipe. There are nearly 200 nesting boxes, cones, and cylinders located throughout the Missisquoi Delta, used by wood duck, common goldeneye, and hooded merganser. Tabor Road offers an open field where white-tailed deer graze spring through fall. Watch for red-tailed and rough-legged hawk, coyote, and red fox. Blueberry picking is permitted during July and August. *BRING INSECT REPELLENT DURING SUMMER MONTHS.*

Directions: *From Swanton, follow Route 78 west for 2.5 miles to refuge headquarters. Tabor Road is 3.3 miles beyond refuge entrance. Turn south on Tabor and follow 0.7 mile to parking on left.*

Closest Town: Swanton

Ownership: USFWS 868-4781

Size: 6,074 acres

Wetlands were once considered unhealthy wastelands. In recent times, marshes, swamps, bogs, and other wetlands are valued for recharging groundwater, cleansing lakes and rivers, and providing buffer zones from flooding and erosion. Wetlands are also the cradle of life for over 600 species of fish, mammals, birds, reptiles, amphibians, and insects.

BLAKE GARDNER

50. SHAD ISLAND AND BIRD'S FOOT DELTA

Description: Bird's Foot Delta is named for the pattern created by three branches of the Missiquoi River as they enter Lake Champlain. Known locally as the West Branch, Middle Branch, and East Branch, these streams resemble the toes on a bird's foot when viewed on a map or from the air.

Viewing Information: Travel by canoe or small boat up the Missisquoi River to see a variety of waterfowl and herons—lucky viewers may see the state-listed endangered spiny softshell turtle. To reach Shad Island, travel on the Middle Branch of the river. The attraction here is one of the largest great blue heron rookeries in the northeast, a colony that may include several hundred birds. Competition for food is great and young herons are known to toss out weaker siblings. To compensate, the adult lays 5-6 eggs, with 2-3 surviving. Nesting takes place during spring and adult herons can be seen flying to the nest, bringing food. They are also very vocal. The large nests sit atop tall trees, making observation from the water quite easy. Binoculars or a spotting scope are highly recommended. *ENTRY ON ISLAND PROHIBITED.*

Directions: *Visit the Missisquoi Wildlife Refuge (site 49) on Route 78 west in Swanton for maps.*

Closest Town: Swanton

Ownership: USFWS 868-4781   **Size:** 114 acres

The heron rookery is unmistakeable, with the stench of rotting fish and excrement, along with the vocalizations of parents and nestlings. A single tree may house several nests as herons tend to colonize, possibly for protection against the red fox and raccoon, or other animals quick to prey upon a fallen nestling.
JOHN HALL

WILDLIFE INDEX

The index below identifies some of the more interesting, uncommon, or popular wildlife found in Vermont, and the best sites for viewing selected species. The numbers following each entry refer to viewing sites, not page numbers.

Amphibians 3, 7, 11, 17, 19, 22, 23, 27, 32, 38, 39, 43, 46, 47-49

Atlantic salmon 1, 5, 16

Beaver 3, 4, 6, 11, 14, 17, 19, 20, 23, 25, 30, 31, 42-44, 47, 49

Black bear 3, 4, 18, 21, 28-34

Common loon 3, 4, 6, 14, 30, 33, 39

Coyote 10, 18, 24, 29, 31, 33, 43, 44, 47, 49

Fish migration 1, 5, 37

Hawk migration 5, 26, 29, 30, 36

Herons 2, 8, 14, 17, 27, 38, 43, 44, 48-50

Mink 2, 6, 10, 23, 30, 39, 42-44, 46

Moose 4, 17, 20, 24, 25, 31-35, 39, 42

Osprey 2, 4, 5, 8, 17, 27, 38, 39, 44, 46-48

Owls 6, 11, 24, 32, 33, 42-44, 47

Peregrine falcon 9, 11, 20, 29, 36

Porcupine 3, 4, 12, 13, 17, 18, 23, 24, 28, 30, 33, 34, 40, 43

Raven 9, 10, 20, 27, 29

River otter 2, 6, 14, 17, 30, 32, 33, 39, 44, 46, 48, 49

Ruffed grouse 4, 8, 22, 24, 31, 32, 43, 44, 47, 48

Warblers 8, 9, 11, 12, 18, 21, 22, 29, 30, 48

Waterfowl migration 5, 8, 10, 14, 22, 26, 27, 30, 38, 43, 44, 46, 49, 50

White-tailed deer 4, 7, 10, 12-14, 17, 18, 21, 22, 24, 25, 28, 31-34, 36, 42, 44, 47-49

Wild turkey 4, 10, 12, 18, 22, 43, 44

Wildlife programs 8, 11, 28, 41, 42

Wildflowers 12, 23, 24, 28, 33, 43

FOR FURTHER READING

The Audubon Society Master Guide To Birding. ed. by John Farrand, Jr., Alfred Knopf; 1983.

Backtracking: The Way of a Naturalist. Ted Levin, Chelsea Green; 1987.

Blood Brook. Ted Levin, Chelsea Green; 1993.

The Book of Forest and Thicket. John Eastman, Stackpole Books; 1992.

Canoe Camping: Vermont and New Hampshire Rivers. Rioli Schweiker, Backcountry Publications; 1989.

Day Hiker's Guide to Vermont. Green Mountain Club; 1992.

Exploring Nature in Winter. Alan M. Cvancara, Walker & Co.; 1992.

The Field Guide to Wildlife Habitats of the Eastern United States. Janine M. Benyus, Simon & Schuster; 1989.

The Nature of Vermont. Charles Johnson, The University Press of New England; 1984.

Peterson's Field Guide to the Mammals. Houghton Mifflin; 1980.

Roadside Geology of Vermont and New Hampshire. Bradford B. Van Diver, Mountain Press; 1992.

Ron Rood's Vermont: A Nature Guide. Ron Rood, The New England Press; 1988.

Tracking and the Art of Seeing. Paul Rezendes, Camden House; 1992.

The Vermont Atlas and Gazetteer. DeLorme Mapping; 1988.

Vermont's Land and Resources. Harold A. Meeks, The New England Press, 1986.

Vermont Guide to Fishing. Vermont Fish and Wildlife Department, 103 South Main St., Waterburg, VT 05676

Vermont Guide to Hunting. Vermont Fish and Wildlife Department, 103 South Main St., Waterburg, VT 05676

Vermont Digest of Fish and Wildlife Laws. Vermont Fish and Wildlife Department, 103 South Main St., Waterburg, VT 05676

WHERE THE WILD THINGS ARE

Falcon Press puts wildlife viewing secrets at your fingertips with our high-quality, full color guidebooks—the Watchable Wildlife series. This is the only official series of guides for the National Watchable Wildlife Program: areas featured in the books correspond to official sites across America. And you'll find more than just wildlife. Many sites boast beautiful scenery, interpretive displays, opportunities for hiking, picnics, biking, plus—a little peace and quiet. So pick up one of our Wildlife Viewing Guides today and get close to Mother Nature!

WATCH THIS PARTNERSHIP WORK

The National Watchable Wildlife Program was formed with one goal in mind: get people actively involved in wildlife appreciation and conservation. Defenders of Wildlife has led the way by coordinating this unique multi-agency program and developing a national network of prime wildlife viewing areas.

Part of the proceeds go to conserve wildlife and wildlife habitat.

Call toll-free or write for a free catalog.

1-800-582-2665

Falcon Press, P.O. Box 1718,
Helena, Montana 59624

FALCON™